CAN'T STOP DANCING

CAN'T STOP DANCING

By

James E Hibbard

BearManor Media
2025

CAN'T STOP DANCING

Published in the United States of America by:

BearManor Media

1317 Edgewater Dr. #110
Orlando, FL 32804

bearmanormedia.com

Printed in the United States.

Typesetting and layout by PKJ Passion Global

ISBN–979-8-88771-646-6

James Hibbard at a dance
recital, 1951

James Hibbard at
International Tap Day, 2019

Preface

My dreams have come true beyond what I could have ever imagined. I have always had a positive nature, and never given much time towards passive or negative thinking. I never planned anything. I just worked hard, and good things came to me. A great friend of mine, Pete Menefee, once told me, "When God was giving out the jaded gene you were at home, sick." I have learned from, and worked with, most of my idols. The guiding angel who made it possible for me to achieve my dreams was my mother, Lois Merle Hibbard. She truly wanted the best for me. Against all early obstacles, she ensured I had the opportunity to succeed. From the moment I started dancing, I have had help and support along the way from an abundance of family, friends, and teachers, but my biggest advocate was my first angel, my mom. I plan to introduce you to as many supporters and mentors as I can remember. They were all my angels. You cannot do this alone. This is my story, as best as I can recall. Jack Pepper, a famous saloon singer and Vaudevillian star, once said, "There is an 'A' version of your story, a 'B' version of your story, and then there is the truth." I will give you my truth as best as I can remember.

Chapter one

My First Angel!

My life has been blessed. My angels have been with me from the moment I was born, and even before. I was born in Klamath Falls, Oregon on July 17, 1943, to Marion Thornton and Lois Merle Hibbard. I had an older brother, Forest Ivan Hibbard (Frosty), who was fourteen months my senior. For the first three years of my life, my brother and I lived in Fort Klamath with our maternal grandparents, Daddy Earle and Grandma Thorpe, as our mom was ill. When she recovered, we joined our parents in Council, Idaho. I had a wonderful childhood. My parents loved us, and I have fond memories of them singing Frosty and me to sleep. They could harmonize and they would sing old Vaudeville love songs to us. Our mom and dad taught us that working hard for what you need and want takes great consistent effort.

Frosty and I spent about ninety-five percent of the time playing outside. We loved western movies, war movies, and gangster movies. We constantly recreated scenarios from movies. Our childhood was filled with magical times. As we grew older, we started arguing and fighting almost every day. Our junior and senior high school years were the worst. We would wrestle and have physical altercations. I was stronger and faster, and would set him into a headlock, punch him, and run. He was slower, and unable to catch me. This behaviour continued until he graduated from high school and went for basic training in the US Air Force. On his return, our fighting briefly resumed. He was now stronger and faster, and, in one fight, he annihilated me. We never fought again. I love him with all my heart. For all our differences, we were alike in spirit. He was a rebel, he went his own way, he never backed down from anything or anyone, and nothing stopped him from getting what he wanted. I love and miss him every day.

My dad was a logger and mechanic. I spent my childhood living in the woods of Idaho in logging camps in Council, Cascade, Idaho City, and Boise, Idaho. I have hunted and fished in stunningly beautiful countryside. My dad taught me the basics of river and stream fishing, but his brother, Uncle Bud, was the true angler. I learned the fine art of trout fishing from him. He once said that I could catch fish even where there were no fish.

I loved my cousins, and we were fortunate to see them quite often. We would visit Uncle Pete and Aunt Virginia's farm to hunt pheasants and ducks, or just to get together. We would travel north to Council, Idaho and visit Uncle Bud, Aunt Pearl, and our cousin Shirley. We played with our cousins Karen, Sheila, Shirley, and Gary until late at night. Gary has since passed, but I am still very close with Sheila and keep in touch with her on Facebook. I am also in touch with my cousin Shirley on Facebook. Shirley is now a successful realtor in New Meadows, Idaho. I am sad to say that I have lost contact with Karen.

My mother used to take my brother and me to see movie musicals in Boise, Idaho. I remember watching Gene Kelly sing and dance in *It's Always Fair Weather* (1954), *Singing in the Rain* (1952), and *American in Paris* (1951). After the movie, my mom said that I would try to dance down the street like Gene Kelly. My brother thought I was nuts, but this gave my mom the idea that I might like dance lessons. She took me to the only dance studio in Boise, the Lillian Winger School of Dance. I started taking tap, ballet, and acrobatics from Lillian and her daughter, Delores. From that moment, I do not remember a time when I did not want to dance. I could not wait for the next class or dance practice. It was not easy for my mom. We lived in a logging camp at Edna Creek, in a primitive area northeast of Boise, Idaho. My mom would drive me two and a half hours to Boise on a Friday evening so that I could take my lessons on Saturday and Sunday. After the lessons, we make the long drive back to the logging camp. In order for me to practice my dancing, my dad and my grandfather pulled a couple of logs into our trailer area and nailed some planks to the logs. I used this rustic floor under the trees to practice my tap and ballet moves.

James Hibbard at a dance recital, 1952

An American in Paris 1951

We eventually moved to Boise, Idaho. My lessons increased, as did my practice time in our garage. I remember taking part in recitals, wearing elaborate costumes made by my mom and grandmother. I remember going to various hospitals, old age homes, and children's hospitals for public performances. I distinctly remember the pleasure I saw in the eyes of the people watching, and how much the joy of entertaining grew in me even at the young age of nine. I still get the same joy of performing. The support of my mom was constant, but my dad did not understand my passion at all. He never saw me dance during all those years. He did not see me dance until after my first professional job, six and a half years later. During those years, I believed my dad did not love me. It was tough on me. He seemed unable to show his love. Through it all, I had my dancing, and, to this day, dancing is the one thing that always saves me.

James Hibbard with three dancing girls

When I was fourteen and a half, my dance teachers came to my mom and dad with a suggestion. We did not know it, but for the past three years my teachers had been going away every summer to further their own dance training. They would bring their new knowledge back and teach it to me. They said I was learning it so fast that it would be a good idea for my parents to take me to New York or Los Angeles to further my training. My dad was immediately against the idea, as money was always a major consideration. My mom persisted until my dad relented. He agreed to pay for my dance lessons for one month on the condition that I take them in West Hollywood, because New York was too far away. My dad said, "At the end of one month, if you are not a star, you are coming home." No pressure, right?

My angel. My mother, Lois Merle Hibbard, 1960

My mom rented a small apartment in West Hollywood for our one-month stay. She contacted the Louis DaPron School of Dance, on La Cienega Boulevard, and set up the number of classes that would fit Dad's budget. Louis DaPron was Donald O'Connor's personal choreographer, as well as a highly respected choreographer in his own right. He worked constantly and was a legend in Hollywood. His timing was near perfect. Louis Dapron was the 'go to guy' to record tap sounds of many of the stars after filming was finished. It was very difficult work, but he was the man. This kind of work is so exacting, and I personally know how hard it is to do. A Rock and Roll band once hired me to record tap sounds to two of their tracks, while they were in Vancouver. It was extremely hard. The requirement was to be on tempo perfectly. It took several takes to get it right. It solidified my respect for that kind of work. The great Louis DaPron dubbed the tap sounds for Gene Kelly, Gene Nelson, Bobby Van, Donald O'Connor, Ann Miller, and others.

Mom and I took a Greyhound bus to Louis DaPron's West Hollywood dance studio. I would repeat this trip to Los Angeles several times before I graduated from High School. I remember the first day we went into Mr. DaPron's studio. He was not there. I auditioned for one of his main teachers, and they recommended many more classes than discussed from Boise, Idaho. I knew we did not have enough money to cover the classes. We left the studio and went for lunch. On the way, my mom stopped at a phone booth on the street and called to ask my dad for more money to cover the increased number of classes. His response was not good. She told me dad had said there was no more money than had originally been planned. We went on our way, planning to have lunch at an Owl Rexall drug store, at the intersection of La Cienega Boulevard and Beverly Boulevard. On the corner before Beverly Boulevard, I noticed a placard on the sidewalk advertising Gene Nelson teaching Tap and Jazz. Gene Nelson was a great song and dance man and had starred, with Doris Day, in many musical movies in the 1950s. He was also one of the stars in the movie *Oklahoma* (1955), playing Will Parker. Gene happened to be one of my idols, so I said, "Ma, let's go in here, please." Going in was the best decision we ever made.

Inside I met a scruffy looking man in bare feet and baggy pants. He had long hair and a heavy key chain coming out of his pocket, which drooped around to a belt loop on his waist. His name was Nico Charisse, the legendary ballet master. Nico designed and built the very first portable ballet bar and sold them out of his school.

Nico Charisse and Marilyn Monroe, 1952

Once a year, Nico would travel in his pickup/camper to dancing schools in the Southwest to guest teach. He would take three or four of his ballet bars and sell them on his way. On one of his earlier trips to the Southwest, he discovered a gifted young dancer in Texas. Her name was Tula Ellice Finklea. Nico encouraged her parents to send her to Los Angeles to train with him. He trained her, introduced her to Hollywood movie studios, and she was quickly noticed by as a bonafide dancing star. She was long legged, and a real beauty and Nico fell in love with her. They were married in 1939, and she changed her name to Cyd Charisse. Nico and Cyd had a son, Nick, and were happy for several years. They divorced in 1947 and she married singer and movie star, Tony Martin.

Nico Charisse and Marilyn Monroe, 1952

Nico Charisse, 1953

Nico Charisse in Paris, France, 1939

I auditioned for Mr. Charisse, and he immediately recognised our financial situation and offered me a ballet scholarship for the month. We would only have to pay for his guest teachers, like Gene Nelson, Sammy Davis, Jr., Lee Scott, and Alex Plasschaert. He gave my mom my one-month schedule. I was exactly where I wanted to be. We walked back up La Cienega Boulevard and canceled the classes at Louis DaPron's School, but my mom then told me we still did not have enough money to meet Nico's suggested number of classes. I understand, now, that in order for Nico not to lose any money I had to take enough classes from his guest teachers to make up for not paying for ballet. We were depressed and decided to continue with our plan to have lunch at Owl Rexall drug store. We went in and noticed a sign indicating an opening for a waitress. My mom had experience being a waitress in a coffee shop when she was young. She seized the day and got the job. This job at the Owl Rexall provided us enough money to pay for the extra lessons needed for the month. The mood of depression evaporated. It seemed life could not be better. Talk about our angels looking out for us. We settled into our little apartment, and I began taking classes the next day. The extra bonus was that I was able to join my mother at the Owl Rexall Cafe for lunch every day, and sometimes even for dinner.

I remember one of my first classes from Gene Nelson. My idea of tap dancing was to tap as fast as I could no matter what the tempo of the music. I was something big in Boise, Idaho, but I learned in a hurry that this was not the case in Hollywood. Gene quickly set me straight and I started to listen carefully to the music. I had developed a habit of counting every beat aloud and snapping my fingers, as I did in Boise. One day Gene turned around and said, "Who is doing that fucking counting and snapping?" I stopped those habits immediately.

A popular hot dog stand, called Tail of the Pup, was next to Nico's studio. Its unique hot dog shape made this stand an iconic Los Angeles landmark. Tail of the Pup became our go-to place to grab bran muffins in between classes. In the 1980s, it was declared a cultural landmark and saved from demolition. It was moved, in its entirety, to a location close to Nico's studio on San Vicente Boulevard.

Tail Of The Pup hot dog stand, 1959

Gene Nelson, 1950

Oklahoma movie poster, 1955

Gene Nelson, 1951

Gene Nelson and Doris Day in *Lullaby of Broadway*, 1951

Gene Nelson in *Oklahoma,* 1955

My one month of dance lessons was over too soon. My father and my brother flew to Los Angeles to meet my mom and me and take us back home. My Dad said to me, "Are you a star?" Of course, my answer was no. He told me that it was time to go home and that I could become a logger, and work with him in his chosen career. My angels must have been watching over me, as they worked their wonder again. When we went to Nico's studio to pay our bill, Nico told my parents that he thought I had a chance in Hollywood, and he offered to take me in. He said that I could live with him and his wife Zita, their son, Marc, and Marc's nanny. His home was on Norwich Avenue in West Hollywood. I could continue with my coveted ballet scholarship, and he would pay me to assist in tap and jazz classes or for work at the studio to help pay for my lessons with his guest teachers. My mom convinced my dad to allow me to try it for a while. This decision started my entire career in show business. I began to stay at Nico's home in West Hollywood for six months, then spend six months at home in Boise, Idaho. I was in seventh heaven!

In West Hollywood, I attended Bancroft Junior High School. They had a professional schedule for artists. I attended Bancroft until 1:00pm each day, and then headed straight to Nico's school for classes. I would take a break for dinner and then head back to the studio for two more dance classes. I repeated this schedule each day. I could not be happier nor in a better atmosphere. I was inspired and motivated. I worked harder than ever.

Chapter Two

Hollywood and Mentors

Six weeks of my new life in Hollywood had passed and my parents and brother were back in Boise, Idaho. My jazz and tap teacher, Gene Nelson, sent me to CBS Studios to audition for his ex-wife, Miriam Nelson. She was choreographing the Jack Benny television series, *Shower of Stars* (1954), a Desilu Production. I do not recall much about the audition but remember there were many boys. The one asset I had, other than being a good dancer, was that I could sing. At fourteen and a half years old, I landed the job. I was hired to sing and dance with The Lennon Sisters. All four Lennon sisters were just beautiful, and I fell in love with each of them, but I had a definite soft spot for Peggy! I can still remember the song we performed. It was "Getting To Know You". My partner was Kathy Lennon, and our show episode was "Comedy Time". It aired live on October 31, 1957, on CBS. A dear friend and colleague, Susan Skemp, recently located the video clip of that number. Amazing!

The Lennon Sisters on Jack Benny's *Shower Of Stars,* 1959

While preparing for the show I went upstairs at CBS studios for school lessons in the morning from 9:00 am until 1:00 pm and then I would run downstairs for rehearsal in the afternoon until 6:00 pm. This schedule went on for a week. Each day, Nico Charisse would drop me off and pick me up. We would have a bite to eat at the Tail of the Pup hotdog stand and then I would take classes from 6:00 pm to 9:00 pm. I could not have been happier. I was completely hooked. If I ever had any doubts about being in show business, which I did not, that was completely over!

People have asked me what it was like performing on my first gig. I do not remember very much. I do remember having a lot of fun. I remember meeting Jack Benny after the show, but what I recall most vividly is that all four Lennon Sisters kissed me good-bye.

I recently saw Miriam Nelson, who gave me that first job, at the Professional Dancer's Society annual luncheon event at the Beverly Hilton Hotel in Beverly Hills. I was surprised that she remembered me. She was receiving her Gypsy Award for her body of choreographic work. I asked her how she was, and she said, "Fine, Jimmy. Just looking for work." She was in her 80s. So inspiring. We planned to meet again at the next Gypsy Awards, but I received the sad news that she had passed away. She was such a lovely lady.

Miriam Nelson, choreographer, 1990

Shortly after my first gig, my friend, actress/dancer, Trudy Ames (nee Ziskind), put me in touch with her agent Hazel Mac-Millan. Hazel was the top agent in Hollywood for kids. Hazel sent me to audition for *Inherit the Wind* (1955) at a local theatre in West Hollywood, and I got the role. The production starred Ted Knight, who later co-starred in the "Mary Tyler Moore Show" (1970), as the weatherman, Ted Baxter.

Ted Knight, 1975

I do not recall much about the part I played, but one memory of the main characters, William Jennings Bryan and Henry Drummond, interrogating me in the centre of the stage stands out. We performed at the Players Ring Gallery, a two hundred-seat theatre in the round, located on Santa Monica Boulevard between Kings Road and Sweetzer Avenue The show received good reviews. Hazel MacMillan came to see the show, and she signed me as a client based on my performance.

Players Ring Gallery Theatre, 1959

I continued a pattern of training for six months in West Hollywood and then spending six months at home in Boise until I graduated from Borah High School in Boise, Idaho in 1961/62. Whenever I was home in Boise, I worked every job I could get in order to save enough money to go back to Hollywood. I worked in the woods as a logger's apprentice, and by the time I was sixteen I had driven my first logging truck. I learned how to cut trees and buck them, cutting them into log lengths. I worked as a soda jerk at a popular drive-in restaurant called, The Howdy Pardner. This job was great fun. The owner of the drive-in was a piano player. On my break, I would go up to the roof that overhung the parked cars. The owner played his piano, and I would tap dance for the patrons as they sat in their cars, munching hamburgers and drinking milkshakes. Instead of applause, the patrons would honk their horns in approval. His drive-in became very popular!

Howdy Pardner drive-in restaurant, 1958

During each of my six months in Hollywood, I worked several jobs in television and stage as an actor/dancer. I landed a recurring role on the series "Mr. Novak" (1963). I had several scenes with the series star, Dean Jagger, who won an Academy Award for Best Supporting Actor in the movie *Twelve O'clock High* (1949). I secured a role on the television series "The Legend Of Jesse James" (1965) and starred in two Heinz Ketchup commercials. I danced in a stage production starring the legendary cowboy singer, Tex Ritter, and I danced and modeled nominated costume designs for the Academy Awards alongside my great friend, Trudi Ames. I also worked a regular job at several restaurants on La Cienega Boulevard, parking patron's cars. La Cienega Boulevard, or Restaurant Row, was lined with popular establishments such as The Captain's Table, and Lawry's Prime Rib. I must have parked every kind of car made. My salary was tiny, but money could be made from the tips the car owners would give. The faster you parked a car, the more money you could make. I wore out the seat of my pants every two weeks from getting in and out of the cars so quickly.

James Hibbard and Trudi Ames at the Academy Awards, 1969

I began teaching tap and jazz classes at the age of sixteen. When Gene Nelson was doing some film or television work, he had me sub for him. It was because of Gene, I humbly became one of the youngest teachers in Hollywood. He had me take over teaching his classes, meaning I have actually been teaching since I was sixteen years old. Other times, Gene had Sammy Davis Jr. sub for him. Sammy had the fastest feet I have ever seen and heard. He would demonstrate difficult combinations and I found it an honour to be able to learn from him.

I decided to spend my senior year at Borah High School in Boise, because I was feeling a bit homesick. It would be fun to be back at school with my friends and just be a normal kid, and graduate at home. My classmates suggested that I run for the position of head cheerleader because of my dancing abilities. They began a political campaign, making signs and I gave out 'Mote For Me' cards to everyone in school. I remember how excited I was awaiting the announcement of results over the homeroom speaker. I was thrilled when I was declared the winner. My crew was made up of four girls, another boy, and me. I choreographed all of the routines and we performed them at all of the football and basketball games.

Baseball season came around and I found myself wanting to play. I successfully tried out for the team. My position was in right field. My dance training helped, especially with timing. As luck would have it, we actually won the state championship. Boise had a major league farm club from the Atlanta Braves, and there happened to be a baseball scout in town during our run for the state championship. He was at our games, and he asked if I would be interested in trying out for the Pittsburgh Pirates. I immediately said yes, and we sat down with my mom and dad to discuss. The scout asked what I wanted to do with my life. I told him that I was a dancer and that was all I ever really wanted to do. He gave me the best advice. He said that his job to offer a career in baseball to talented players, but he warned it would not be easy. He said all of the players coming in to try out would be taller, bigger, could run faster, hit harder, and jump higher. He said I should have a serious talk with my parents and make a decision. His advice was the right advice. I liked playing baseball, but I loved to dance more. He said that I made the right decision and wished me well. This man was another angel in my life.

I danced all over Boise and the surrounding communities. I had proven myself with getting work in my chosen profession and my dad finally came around and accepted my love of dancing. He even had me dance for his colleagues and co-workers at their annual year-end conventions. I appreciated all of the time he supported me with paying for my lessons, but I still yearned for him to show his love for me.

My mom and dad, 1965

Nico Charisse

Ballet Master, Dancer, Choreographer, Mentor

Nico Charisse saved my professional life. He stepped in when my dad was going to take me back to Boise, Idaho following my month of dance lessons at his studio. My dad's intentions were to have me become a logger and to work in construction with him.

Nico told my parents he thought I had a chance in show business. I could continue my training and stay with him and his family. I owe him a great debt of gratitude for his foresight and generosity. Without him, I do not know what would have happened to me. I honour him every day.

Nico Charisse was born in Athens, Greece on March 1, 1906. Nico was the second oldest of eleven children. Nico's mother, Calliope Charisse (1880-1946), was a famous interpretive dancer inspired by Isadora Duncan. She and her children performed in Greece, Europe and the United States. Nico, his brother Noel, his sister Nanette, and the rest of his family were all part of a mini ballet troupe.

Nico Charisse Family Ballet Company, 1923

During World War I, they toured Europe performing condensed versions of ballets for the troops. In 1923, the family immigrated to the United States and continued to perform at different venues. They became stars at the Hippodrome and on the B.F. Keith circuit, a chain of Vaudeville theatres in the United States and Canada.

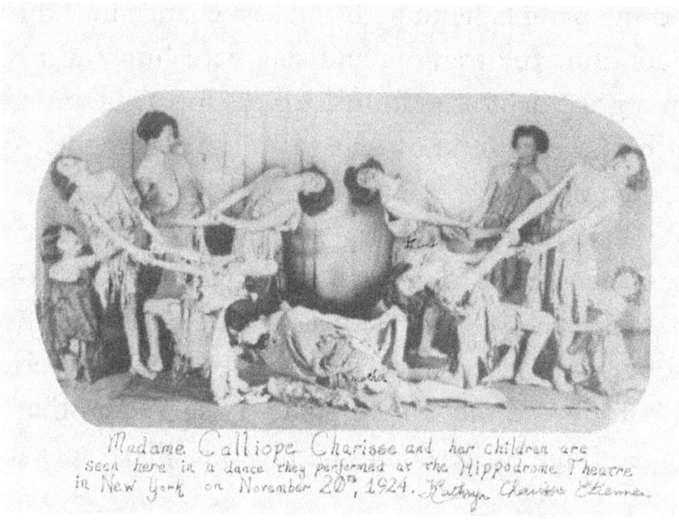

Nico Charisse Family Ballet Company at The Hippodrome, 1924

Dancing movie star, Cyd Charisse, studied with Nico Charisse in Los Angeles. They met again while dancing together with Les Ballet Russes, which was on tour in Europe. In 1939, they married in Paris, France. Their son, Nick, was born in 1942. They divorced in 1947. Nico remarried on February 7, 1953, to Zita Torres. Nico and Zita had one son together, Marc. Cyd remarried Tony Martin, a singing movie star in his own right.

Cyd and Nico Charisse, 1939

Nico Charisse Jr., 2015

Marc Charisse, 2018

In 1943 Nico was choreographer on the movie *The Sultan's Daughter* (1943), produced by Monogram and Philip N. Krasne Productions and directed by Arthur Dreifuss. The movie starred Ann Ryan, Charles Butterworth and Irene Ryan. Irene went on to play the character Granny in the television show *The Beverly Hill-*

billies (1962). Years later, I danced in "Hoe Down A Go Go" from season four of *The Beverly Hillbillies* (1962).

Movie poster from *The Sultan's Daughter,* 1943

Movie poster from *The Sultan's Daughter,* 1943

Nico was my ballet master and surrogate father during my time living with him and his family at their home in West Hollywood. Nico was the best all around dance teacher I have ever studied with. His wife, Zita, was also a sensational teacher. She was responsible for my regular technical classes. She was a taskmaster. I thought she drove me too hard, but everybody felt the same way. She was responsible for helping me improve my technical ability, which rounded out the dancer I was and became. I loved her then, but I think of her now with even greater love and respect. With Nico's mentorship and Zita's technical teaching, my dancing became better and more refined. The training by Nico's extraordinary guest teachers, Gene Nelson, Lee Scott, Maurice Kelly, Nanette Charisse, Alex Plasschaert, Dick Humphries, and Sammy Davis Junior, molded me into the dancer I have become.

I loved living with Nico and his family. Their house on Norwich Avenue, in West Hollywood, was full of love. There was always something creative happening there. We would lay new dance floors or build a new float for a parade down Hollywood Boulevard. Nico would carve ballet figurines or construct portable ballet bars to sell at his school. Below is a photo of Nico showing one of his figurines to Marilyn Monroe at the studio. I remember watching Nico carving the figurines at the dining room table just like this one. He had such a talent.

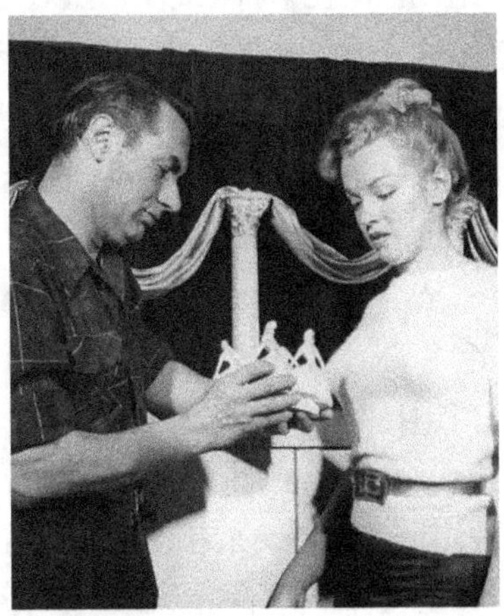

Nico Charisse showing his figurines to Marilyn Monroe, 1949

Nico Charisse showing his figurines to Marilyn Monroe, 1949

Zita's mother lived in Beverly Hills and had an enormous avocado tree in her garden. We would go there once a week, climb up the tree, and pick the most beautiful huge avocados for our weekly supply. Nico and Zita had two dogs, a German Short-Haired Pointer named Sybella and a miniature poodle named Tonic. Sybella was at Nico's side all the time, and Tonic was Zita's dog. Sybella usually came with us to the studio and would sit quietly at Nico's side in the pickup truck and lay right at Nico's feet while he taught ballet class. Tonic had an amazing habit. After dancing most of the day, we would come home and the first thing we did was take our shoes off. Tonic loved to lick feet. I know it sounds crazy, but it was such wonderful relief. That little dog was a blessing.

Nico and Cyd's son, Nick, and I became the best of friends. I would stay at Nico's home in West Hollywood most of the time, but occasionally stay at Cyd Charisse's home, in Beverly Hills, with Nick. It was two distinctly different worlds. Nico's modest home was full of life, laughter, and artistic people. Cyd's very posh estate in Bel Air was full of new cars but had a very cold atmosphere.

Nico and Zita's son, Marc, had a nanny named Suzanne. I remember her being affectionate to Marc, but she was very strict with me. Marc was just a young boy when I lived with them. I have recently made contact with Marc through Facebook. He and his family live in Pennsylvania. He is a professional magician, a builder of magic boxes, teacher and lecturer in Mass Communications at York College. I enjoy speaking with him. He is a gentleman. I understand he and his wife are accomplished ballroom dancers. It is true that the apple does not fall far from the tree.

To look at Nico, you would never guess he was a ballet master. He wore baggy pants with the cuffs rolled up, a long key chain from his belt into his pocket, a loose shirt, long hair, he was always bare footed, and he carried a walking stick. During class, he would sometimes get up and demonstrate a ballet combination. You would not believe the transformation. He danced so beautifully. When finished, he would stop and shuffle back to his seat in front of the class. He was a character. Nico had no pretensions at all. He always had a smile ready, no ego, had a real twinkle in his eyes, and was always giving. Nico made me feel comfortable in class. He said I could wear any clothing I wanted to as long as it did not restrict my movements. I was young and embarrassed about wearing tights, and I did not have to wear ballet shoes. I usually just wore my socks, or my lightweight Tretorn running shoes. Nico just wanted me to concentrate on dancing.

Another of Nico's talents was as a photographer. All of his students, myself included, had him take photos of us dancing. He framed them and hung them all over the school. Some of us used the photos professionally to get dance jobs. Nico's photos were my resume photos in the beginning of my career when money was tight. Here are a few he took of me.

James Hibbard photographed by Nico Charisse, 1958

James Hibbard photographed by Nico Charisse, 1958

James Hibbard photographed by Nico Charisse, 1958

James Hibbard photographed by Nico Charisse, 1958

Nico was so charming. All of the women loved him. Zita, his wife, was the organizer and the business head of the family. They were a great balancing act for each other. His class assistant was Rosemarie Biensfeld, a gorgeous ballet dancer. I was smitten with her, but she was dating Nico's son, Nick. Nick and I had become the best of friends, so there could be no romantic involvement there. Each time I go to Los Angeles, I make time to visit with Rosemarie. She still calls me one of her boys, which is flattering.

Almost every female movie star took private lessons from Nico. Ava Gardner, Marilyn Monroe, Jean Simmons, Ann Miller, and Shirley MacLaine all worked with him. Every dancer in the business studied under him at some time or another. One day, Nico sent Zita and me to the set of the 1960 Academy Award winning film, *Elmer Gantry* (1960), to give a private ballet lesson to star, Jean Simmons. I ended up teaching Ms. Simmons myself while Zita was busy at Nico's studio. She was a wonderful and gracious lady. She introduced me to her co-star, Academy Award winner for Best Actor, Burt Lancaster.

Nico's younger students were also in the movies. Next time you watch *White Christmas* (1954), keep an eye out for the little ballerina right up front in the finale. Her name is Randy Rayburn. She was one of Nico's students from his Pony class. Any dancer who was accepted into Nico's Pony class were the best female dancers at the school. Randy was no exception. She had infinite talent, but no desire for a career in dance. She gave up dancing a few years after *White Christmas* (1954).

I remember one day, in 1963, Nico asked me to give a young girl a private jazz lesson. As I was finishing the hour lesson, I noticed a man standing in the doorway watching. I couldn't see his face as he was backlit from the sunshine beaming into the studio. At the end of the lesson, the man came out onto the floor and introduced himself to me. He shook my hand and told me how much he appreciated my style of teaching, and how kind I was to this girl. His name was Groucho Marx. The young girl was his daughter, Melinda. I was speechless.

Nico's talents were endless. He had designed most of his entire dance studio. One of his ingenious design features turned his big ballet studio in the back of the building into a theatre. His private dance studio in the middle of the school had one wall that opened to become a stage, facing his studio. It was 6 steps up from the ballet floor. It was equipped with lights, curtains, and wings for entrances. There were chairs hidden inside one wall of the ballet studio that were brought out for the audience to sit on. This is where we put on special presentations and recitals.

At one of those special presentations, Maurice Kelly, my current tap teacher, asked me to perform a dance with a very special guest. Mr. Kelly just happened to be the personal choreographer for this guest. His name was Ray Bolger. He played the Strawman in the classic movie, *The Wizard of Oz* (1939). Mr. Bolger was a great showman. He was very patient with me and extremely supportive. Although I was barely sixteen years old, I picked up quickly and he really appreciated that. We sang and danced to "Me And My Shadow". Of course, I was the Shadow. It was one of the most wonderful moments of my dancing life.

Ray Bolger, 1939

Ray Bolger, 1942

Ray Bolger and Judy Garland in *Wizard of Oz*, 1939

Everything I learned from Nico, Zita, and the guest teachers, I continue to use to this very day. In 1965, I was dancing in the movie *Marriage On The Rocks* (1965), starring Frank Sinatra, Dean Martin, Deborah Kerr, and Nancy Sinatra. Once, during a break, the choreographer, Jonathan Lucas, asked if any of us dancers knew the current dances of the 60's. I had just finished choreographing and dancing on Dick Clark's hit television series, *Where The Action Is* (1965), which was all about the current dances and recording artists in the 60s. My hand shot up and I said, "Yes!" To my surprise, he came right over to me and said, "Come with me." As we made our way to the set, he told me that he wanted me to teach one of the actors how to dance the Swim. The actor's name was Frank Sinatra. I admit, I freaked out a little.

This is where my training from Nico supported me. Nico taught me that there are a million ways to get from A to B, when teaching someone a move or dance they are completely unfamiliar with. That training saved my bacon. I calmed down and remembered Nico's words. He had taught me to find an action or movement that the person can relate to, that resembles the movement you want them to do. I knew Mr. Sinatra liked boxing, so I started having him do a very slow speed bag punching movement. I then had him open up his hands, and before long he was doing the front swim stroke to the music. When he was relaxed, I gave him other swim moves. I taught him a move called the Bugaloo, which resembles milking a cow, but with bigger movements. The moves were similar to the Monkey. He thought it was hysterical. He successfully performed the dance in a go-go cage with his daughter, Nancy Sinatra. He looked good, comfortable, and relaxed, and was very complimentary to me. I remember Nico's words to me, "You have to park your ego outside and make sure your student looks good, naturally. It doesn't matter what they do. If they look good, you look good." These are words I live by.

In 1965 Nico and Zita moved to Las Vegas, where he continued to teach out of his home. He was involved with some professional dance projects there. After they moved to Las Vegas, I lost contact with them. I regret that to this day. I was so busy working, but that is not an important enough reason. I owed them more. Nico and Zita saved my professional life and became my surrogate parents during the time I lived with them. In 1970, Nico died of a heart attack. Their son, Marc, said his mother never danced again after his death. Zita passed away in 2006. Marc told me he had inherited a property from Nico and Zita, located in northern Washington State. He and his family are thinking about moving there in about a year. If they do, we will surely get together and catch up. Nico and Zita live on in my mind and heart. I miss them every day.

Gene Nelson

Gene Nelson, 1952

Gene Nelson was a star of stage, screen, and television, and was a screenwriter and director. Gene was born Leander Eugene Berg on March 24, 1920, in Astoria Oregon. At the age of one, he and his family moved to Seattle, Washington. It is said that Gene was barely a teenager when he saw Fred Astaire dance in the film *Flying Down to Rio* (1933). This film changed Gene's life. It was at this moment that he decided he would be a dancer. This life changing moment was similar to my experience after watching *It's Always Fair Weather* (1955), with Gene Kelly. Another interesting experience we had in common was that, in high school, Gene organized and rehearsed a cheering squad for football games. I was the head cheerleader at my school for football and basketball games. We certainly had similar beginnings.

Gene joined the Army during World War II, touring with Irving Berlin's *This is the Army* (1943), entertaining troops all over Europe. After the war, Gene secured a two-year contract with 20th Century Fox. At Warner Bros., Gene starred with Doris Day in several films, including *Lullaby of Broadway* (1951) and *Tea for Two* (1950). I should mention that Doris Day had and amazing dancing ability that has been overlooked. She truly was a gifted dancer.

Gene Nelson and Doris Day in *Lullaby of Broadway*, 1951

Gene Nelson and Doris Day in *Tea for Two*, 1950

Gene is most recognized for his role in *Oklahoma* (1955), where he played Will Parker. I was twelve years old when I saw *Oklahoma* (1955), and Gene immediately became one of my idols. He was an immense talent, gifted on stage, screen, and television. Gene excelled at everything he did. He sang, danced, was an amazing gymnast, acted, directed, produced, and wrote screenplays. He won a Golden Globe Award in 1951 for Best Newcomer, and his star is on the Hollywood Walk of Fame.

Gene Nelson in *Oklahoma,* 1955

Gene Nelson was soon in demand for guest starring roles following his success in the movie *Oklahoma* (1955). He would frequently bring in substitute teachers to teach us while he was away doing his gigs. I met several people I would work with later in various film, television, and stage projects. People such as Sammy Davis, Jr., Alex Plasschaert, Ray Bolger, Lee Scott, Maurice Kelly, Earl Barton, and Roland Dupree to name a few. These were prodigiously talented people. My good fortune just simply rolled on and on.

Gene Nelson, 1956

Gene Nelson directing on set of *Kissin Cousins*, 1964

Gene Nelson, 1956

Gene Nelson was a major mentor in my life. He helped me get my first professional job, and he started me in my teaching career. In a few years Gene Nelson was firmly into his directing career and I had the pleasure of working with him in two films. In 1964, he directed the Elvis Presley movie *Kissin Cousins* (1964), for MGM Studios. Hal Belfer choreographed and my friend, Pete Menefee, assisted Mr. Belfer. I sang and danced in that film. It was a great reunion for Gene and me. In 1967, Gene directed the movie *The Cool Ones* (1967), for Warner Bros. Studio. The movie was choreographed by Toni Basil, and I assisted her. I sang and danced in it and had the opportunity for another reunion with Gene. As a special treat, I got to drive Gene's car in the movie. It was a red and white 1965 Mustang convertible, one of my all-time favorite cars.

James Hibbard in *The Cool Ones,* 1967

James Hibbard in The Cool Ones, 1967

James Hibbard in The Cool Ones, 1967

Following our work on *The Cool Ones* (1967), I never had the opportunity to work with Gene again. In his magnificent career he directed fifty-four television and film projects, and starred in sixty-six films, stage, and television shows. This in addition to him writing screenplays, recording, and producing. He demanded that I work hard and was a great task master. He encouraged me to teach when I was sixteen years old. When he left Nico's school, I inherited his classes. Gene died in 1996, and I think of him every day. He generously furthered my career several times and showed that he was genuinely happy for me each time we met. I loved this man. He was a major angel in my life.

Gene Nelson, 1990.

I did not know it then, but I had the best dance training that I could possibly get. I was lucky, at such a young age, to know what I wanted to do. My mom and dad taught me that hard work brings good results. I had the best teachers and mentors, including my parents, guiding me every step of the way. Everything that was given to me prepared me for all that was to come.

Here is one truth. I was a worker bee. I just kept working. I was star struck. I loved show business as I knew it. I never marketed myself. I never thought about it. I just kept going. I knew my angels were with me and never worried about not working. I never analyzed anything. There were times when I was strapped for money, but I never let it get me down. I always knew something would come up. I kept my spirits up by taking classes at Nico Charisse's studio, at Roland Dupree's School, and with Eugene Loring. I taught at both Roland Dupree's School and at Nico's studio, parked cars at most of the restaurants on Restaurant Row, such and hustled snooker games at Mother's Pool Hall. This enabled me to pay bills until a job came through. Toni Basil, dear friend, gifted choreographer, film maker, and visionary, gave me as much work as she could.

To me it was a great life. This was everything I ever dreamed of. This was the way it was supposed to be. I had my first agent for acting, Hazel MacMillan, who got me a fair amount of work. She was a smart cookie and a classy lady. I knew that the only way to go was forward and go forward was exactly what I did. There was no other option. I bless my parents for this attitude. I knew I had my dream and good things would come my way. After all this time, I am still that worker bee. I am still star struck. I still love show business. I am still working, but most of all I have always been and still am a dancer.

James Hibbard at International Tap Day, 2018

Chapter Three

Gypsy

In 1961, after I graduated from Borah High School in Boise, Idaho, I boarded the Greyhound bus for the last time and headed back to Hollywood. I rented my first apartment in the Hollywood Hills for the hefty sum of $65 per month and began life on my own.

I continued to train at Nico's school and picked up teaching gigs every chance I could. My parents would send me a little bit of money whenever they could. One day, my dad decided that I was on my own and I should grow up and fend for myself. He refused to send me any more money. He said that was what he had to do in his life, and I should do the same. I hated him for that, but reality helps you grow up quickly. I was truly on my own. I never asked for money again, although my mother would sometimes sneak some money to me.

Prospects for work looked a little bleak, having just arrived from Idaho. I was taking a jazz class at a Hollywood dance studio with a great dancer named Nick Navarro. He told all of us in class that there was an audition at his studio coming up in about a week. It was for a job in Las Vegas. I had never been to Las Vegas and was excited to try out. The audition was for the *Phil Harris Show* (1954), at the Desert Inn Hotel. Phil Harris was an actor/comedian/singer. He was married to a beautiful film star, Alice Faye. The act was to be choreographed by Dick Humphreys, a wonderful tap dance artist who had danced in many Gene Kelly films. I met a female dancer/actor, Lesley Evans, at the audition and we both got the job along with six other dancers. We were given beautiful rooms at the Desert Inn during the rehearsals. Dick, our choreographer, had a featured tap dance solo in the show. Every night I watched Dick dazzle the audience with his magical feet and stage presence. I was so impressed with his tap-dancing wizardry. He really connected with the audience. I wanted to dance just like him. To this very day I still remember some of his routine and include parts of his dance whenever I perform.

Another act in Phil Harris's show was a young elephant, painted pink. Mr. Harris would put the elephant through some tricks. The audience loved it. One night, the elephant had enough of being put through his paces so close to the audience. He panicked, ran off the stage towards the audience, and plowed through tables and chairs. Terrified people were sent scurrying all over, while the elephant ran out of the showroom, into the casino, and out to the parking lot. This was the last time elephant act was featured in the show.

I had an experience during our run that profoundly moved me. On closing night Phil's wife, Alice Faye, was in the audience. After taking our bows, she suddenly came on stage and walked right over to me. She took my face in her hands, looked into my eyes, and said, "I can see it in your eyes. You are going to do great things." Then she kissed me on both cheeks. It was one of those times when someone, anyone, says something to you which affirms that you are on the right track, exactly when you needed it most. She was an angel. I still see her beautiful face with startling blue eyes looking right at me. We all need these moments every once in a while.

Alice Faye and Phil Harris, 1964

Dick Humphries hired me to dance in another lounge act, the *Louis Prima Show* (1954), at the Thunderbird Hotel. In this show, my dance partner was the beautiful, talented dancer/actress, Lesley Evans. To this day, Lesley remains one of my best friends. We were featured dancers in the show doing Dick's choreographed version of the current dance craze, the Twist.

I recently came across a video of Dick dancing with Gene Kelly and another teacher/mentor of mine, Alex Plasschaert. They were doing a trio performance of a famous tap dance number from Vaudeville called The Chain Dance, on the television series *Hollywood Palace* (1964). It was moving to see my idol, Gene Kelly, along with two of my teacher/mentors dancing together.

Gene Kelly, Alex Plasschaert, and Dick Humphreys
at Hollywood Palace, 1964

After we closed the *Louis Prima Show* (1954), in Las Vegas, Dick Humphreys called and asked Lesley and me if we wanted to dance for him in a movie starring Louis Prima and June Wilkinson. He would put us together as a pair and feature us. We did not have to audition. The film's working title was *The Continental Twist* (1961), which later became *Twist All Night* (1961). We both jumped at the opportunity.

To dance in the movie, we had to become members of Screen Extras Guild. This was not easy. Dick decided to sponsor us and swore to Screen Extras Guild that Lesley and I were the King and Queen of the Twist. That was not enough to satisfy the Guild. They insisted he hold a major audition for dancers to prove we were what he said we were. He held the audition and made the choreography very difficult. Lesley and I had his style down. When Screen Extras Guild saw a video of us doing Dick's version of the Twist, we were accepted. This illustrates the kind of person Dick Humphreys was. He was kind, generous, and always giving. I love and miss him. *Twist All Night* (1961) was released about forty-eight hours before Chubby Checker's famous movie *Twist Around The Clock* (1961). Despite Louis Prima's movie being released first, Chubby Checker's movie was infinitely more popular.

James Hibbard in *Twist All Night,* 1961

After finishing principal filming of Louis Prima's *Twist All Night* (1961) movie, I was in the union, on cloud nine, and raring to go. I purchased my first car from a friend of mine, Irwin Berniker. It was a Fiat and I paid $200. What a great purchase. This was good timing because I needed a car to get to my next job, a stage musical starring Milo O'Shea for the Bakersfield Civic Light Opera. Jack Bunch produced, directed, and choreographed it. He had seen Milo performing in Ireland and brought him over to do the show. The rest is history. Milo O'Shea's career took off in America and he became a prolific star of stage, screen, and television. He also was nominated twice for Tony Awards on Broadway.

Bakersfield, California is 111 miles from Hollywood. On my first drive to rehearsal, the Fiat caught fire and literally burned up on the side of the freeway, 50 miles outside of Los Angeles. I guess it was not such a good purchase. While I was waiting for the car to be towed, another cast member, Bert Michaels, stopped and gave me a ride to rehearsal. Bert played one of the Jets in *West Side Story* (1961). The police told me that they would be in touch with me, but I never heard from them. I did hear from the insurance company. They covered the costs of towing my Fiat straight to the auto graveyard. My angels were really looking out for me.

When I finished this job, I decided to move to a better apartment. I found a garage that had been converted into a suite, just behind a house a block from Nico's home on Norwich Avenue. It was great. I was close to Nico and his school. I guess I needed to be close to my surrogate family. I also bought a good car. It was a 1962 Ford Galaxie. It was a beautiful red and white convertible. I was going to go to my next job in style.

Amazingly, within a week, I heard about a dance audition in the Hollywood Reporter and the Variety trade papers. These were our Bibles because all auditions were posted in them. One of the postings was for a job dancing on a weekly television series called *Polka Parade* (1955), at KTLA Channel 5 studios. I auditioned and got the job. The only dances we did on the show were Polkas. We would rehearse for four hours on Sunday morning and learn six or seven different Polka dances and perform them live on Sunday evening. The sponsor was Farmer John Sausages. My pay was $75 a week, and a Farmer John ham, some sausages, or turkey as a bonus. What a crazy job! The Polkas were hard to remember because they were all the same, with only minor changes. I worked on the show from October to December. In December, just before Christmas, the producer told me he was going to replace me with his brother's son, who needed a job. I was devastated! They gave me my pay, a turkey, and a bottle of Jack Daniels Bourbon. I went to Nico's house, gave them the turkey for Christmas, and Nico, Zita, Noel, Nico's brother and I cracked open the bottle of whiskey. I can say with authority that in my whole life, I have never been as drunk as I was that night. I was not a drinker and it showed.

Publicity Poster for *Polka Parade*, 1951

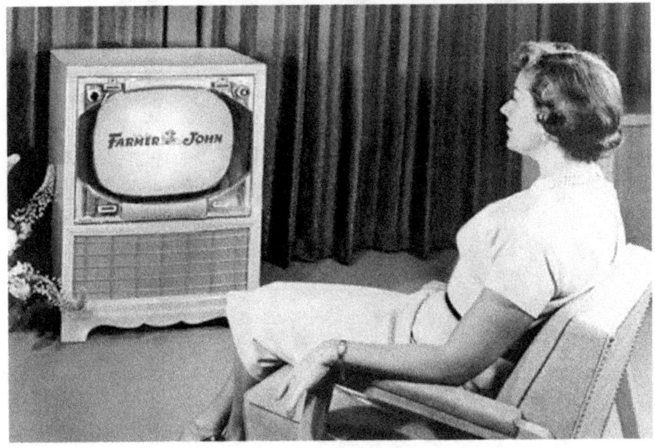

Publicity Poster for *Polka Parade*, 1951

Publicity Poster for *Polka Parade,* 1951

1961 ended with me being fired from a job. This was the only job I was ever fired from. I was upset, but most of all I was embarrassed. I didn't know it then, but a magical time was just around the corner. My momentous start to 1962 was landing my first movie musical, starring in *Gypsy* (1962).

Poster from *Gypsy,* 1962

I was taking a tap class from Alex Plasschaert at Nico's studio, when Nico came in and pulled me out of class. He said that his sister, Nanette, was in town and she had mentioned there was a dance audition I might be right for. The audition was coming up at Warner Bros. studios. Nanette's husband, Robert Tucker, was the choreographer. The project was the movie, *Gypsy* (1962), starring Natalie Wood, Rosalind Russell, and Karl Malden. Mervyn Leroy was set to produce and direct. *Gypsy* (1962) was a story about the famous burlesque performer, Gypsy Rose Lee, and her rise to stardom. The audition was held on the back lot of Warner Bros. Studios in an old house. There were hundreds of male dancers of various ages trying out. We were taught tap sequences, staging sequences, and we had to sing. One of the songs we were taught still rings in my ears.

Broadway, Broadway, we've missed it so.
We're leaving soon and taking June, to star her in a show.
Bright lights, white lights, rhythm and romance.
The train is late, so while we wait, we're going to do a little dance!

I was cast as one of the farm boys, in coveralls and straw hats, with Dainty June and her singing/dancing cow. I did get to change things up in the *Broadway Eton* (1962) number, getting dressed up in a spiffy tux and top hat. I was where I wanted to be.

James Hibbard and Paul Wallace in *Gypsy*, 1962

James Hibbard in *Gypsy*, 1962

Scene from *Gypsy*, 1962

I have many memories from working on this film, but this one certainly stands out in my mind and will not leave. During the rehearsal period, I had the extremely pleasurable shock of seeing Natalie Wood half naked. We rehearsed in the same old house on the back lot that we auditioned in. One day, on my way back from lunch at the studio commissary, I decided to take a shortcut through the back of the house, and I interrupted Ms. Wood while she was having a costume fitting in a back room. She was naked from her waist up. I was so embarrassed and apologized profusely. She did not say anything, just covered herself up. A week later, I came back from lunch, through the back of the building, and walked into another costume fitting for Natalie. This time, she was naked from her head to her toe. I froze and she said, calmly, "Jimmy, we have to stop meeting like this!" She did not even try to cover herself up. I loved her from that moment on. Every day after this she would make a point of greeting me with, "Hi Jimmy," whenever we were in rehearsal or on set. She was so beautiful and kind. She definitely got a kick out of my embarrassment.

Natalie Wood in *Gypsy*, 1962

While filming *Gypsy* (1962), I met the wonderful Paul Wallace, who played Tulsa. He also created the role in the original Broadway production with Ethel Merman. I used to watch him rehearse his feature number *All I Need Is The Girl* (1959) with Ms. Wood. I was so impressed with his work. I watched every time he rehearsed. Several days, during lunch, I stayed in the rehearsal space and ran through his number by myself over and over until I had it down cold. One day, he came back early and caught me doing his number. He was not pleased and told me so, in no uncertain terms. I apologized and told him it was because I admired him so. In truth, he was doing what I wanted to do some day. He understood and we became great friends from that day on. We spent time together for about a year after the movie was completed before going our separate ways.

Paul Wallace, 1962

One day, while filming, we had a special guest. It was none other than the real Miss Gypsy Rose Lee! The stage play and the movie are based on her book *Gypsy: A Memoir* (1957). I remember her being not only beautiful, tall, and glamorous, but elegant, kind, and appreciative of all of us. Here are a few photographs of her with Natalie Wood. It was a special day.

Natalie Wood and Gypsy Rose Lee on set of *Gypsy,* 1962

Natalie Wood and Gypsy Rose Lee on set of *Gypsy*, 1962

Natalie Wood and Gypsy Rose Lee on set of *Gypsy*, 1962

I loved working on this film. My contract was for six weeks. I felt like I earned a fortune. My pay was $344 per week under Screen Actors Guild guidelines. It was quite a jump from $65 per week, plus a ham, while working on *Polka Parade* (1955). I also met a new friend, fellow dancer Dick Foster, but I will tell you more about him later.

As a farm boy, I did not have any scenes with Karl Malden, but working with Rosalind Russell was great fun. During the big finale to the farmboys number, with Dainty June, we would be in costumes of tuxedos and top hats. Ms. Russell, in her character as Mama Rose, would yell from the wings to keep our dancing lines straight. If one of us dropped our top hat, she would run out on stage, to pick it up, while we were trying to finish the dance. She was improvising because she did not know where she was going to be. Of course, the hat was being kicked around. As my good fortune would have it, she was right in front of me when I had to dance quickly from upstage to downstage. As I was adjusting to go around her, she whispered to me, "Sorry, Jimmy." It all worked out, but it was frantic for a while. She was so gracious. Working with Ann Jillian, as Dainty June, was a real treat. I remember her as being so prepared, professional, friendly, and always on her marks. She was a gem, and so pretty.

James Hibbard and Rosalind Russell in *Gypsy*, 1962

Gypsy, 1962

In my mind, being in *Gypsy* (1962) would have satisfied me for all of 1962. However, my angels had much more in mind for me. Through my agent, Hazel MacMillan, I landed a one-line role on the *Tales of Wells Fargo* (1957) television series. I also got an acting part with Hayley Mills, for a Disney television special. I played her boyfriend, and we took the audience on tour through the many features of Disneyland in Anaheim, California. Following this, I danced in a musical revue starring Tex Ritter. Tex Ritter was a cowboy singer who sang the theme song *Do Not Forsake Me* (1952) from the movie *High Noon* (1952), starring Gary Cooper. That song was the first Oscar winning song from a non-musical movie. Tex Ritter is also the father of John Ritter, star of the hit television series *Three's Company* (1977).

Nico Charisse's sister, Nanette, was giving a master class in ballet while she was in town. Nico insisted that I take her class. Several of the dancers in *Gypsy* (1962) were going, plus dancers from many other schools in Los Angeles. To this day, I remember the class and how extremely difficult it was. She was a tactician of the highest order. I've never had a more intensive class ever. Her class concentrated on balance and turns. We had to balance on one foot, raise up onto the ball of the foot, and hold still. She would say, "Turn," without any preparation. To our surprise, it began to work. By the smallest of movement, we started to slowly turn while on balance. Some of us made it all the way around. Once we found our own balance point, it seemed so easy. By the end of class, we were all doing three and four pirouettes with relative ease. I've never had a similar class since. Her voice still rings loudly. I remember her teachings. She was a great teacher.

Throughout those years, I always returned to take classes. Classes at Nico's studio, classes with Roland Dupree at his studio, classes from Nick Navarro in Hollywood, plus classes from beautiful film star, Juliet Prowse. I took classes anywhere and everywhere. It was an effective way to market yourself, being seen in as many places as possible. The added bonus was staying in shape, ready for the next opportunity.

Chapter Four

Bye Bye Birdie

All my work in 1961 and 1962 was back-to-back. It was an exciting two years. To say I was busy would be an understatement. I was working, I was on the top of the wave, and I was eating up every moment of it. Movies, television, and stage were on the menu.

Movie poster for *Bye Bye Birdie*, 1963

Sandwiched in between all of the work, in late Spring, I auditioned for the film *Bye Bye Birdie* (1963), for Columbia Pictures. The choreographer was Onna White, who later won an Academy Award for her choreographic work on the film *Oliver* (1968). The audition was great fun. I enjoy auditions very much. I always have. At auditions I knew I had a good chance to succeed and get the job, because I kept my chops up and I was ready. Every free time I had, I got back into class. I never worried about being able to do the work. I knew I could do it. It just boiled down to whether I was the right type or not. My being confident in my ability made it a much easier, enjoyable process.

Every dancer in Hollywood was at the audition at a sound stage on the Universal Studios lot. The process took hours and hours, and we did not finish it in one day. We had two more days of callbacks before they decided on who they wanted. Finally, I received the good news. I had landed one of the long jobs I had heard about. Long jobs are few and far between. Most jobs are from one to eight weeks at the most. When I started to work in films, seasoned dancers told me, "One day, Jimmy, you too will get a long job." These dancers had been in famous dance films such as *Seven Brides for Seven Brothers* (1954), *Li'l Abner* (1959), and *Westside Story* (1961). On these films they had worked anywhere from four months to one and a half years. I worked on *Bye Bye Birdie* (1963) for about four months, so it qualified for a long job status. It seemed like longer, but it was spread out from the auditions and the shooting schedule from June through September of 1962.

Bye Bye Birdie (1963) was based on the 1960 Tony Award winning Broadway stage production, co-starring Ann-Margret, Dick Van Dyke and Janet Leigh. This movie was directed by George Sidney, produced by Fred Kohlmar, and distributed by Columbia Pictures. The character of Conrad (Birdie), played by Jesse Pearson along with the story was inspired by Elvis Presley being drafted into the United States Army in 1957. *Bye Bye Birdie* (1963) was nominated for two Academy Awards and two Golden Globes.

We started rehearsals in mid 1962. I was in heaven. I was nineteen, playing a seventeen-year-old in his senior year in High School. It was extra fun to play close to my age. I met Ann-Margret for the first time and fell in love with her. I am still in love with her, and I know that I am not alone in that. I did not know it then, but I was destined to work with Ann-Margret four more times after we finished *Bye Bye Birdie* (1963). In 1964, we worked together in *Viva Las Vegas* (1964), with Elvis Presley. In 1966, we joined forces in

The Swinger (1966), with Anthony Franciosa, and in 1967, I worked with Ann-Margret at her first night club act in Las Vegas. Finally, in 1969, I was part of her television special featuring her Las Vegas act. I will tell you all about these jobs later in the book.

During the rehearsal and filming of the "Honestly Sincere" (1963) number at the Universal Studios town square set, we were given a break. Ann-Margret, along with a couple of girls, asked if I wanted to take a walk with them on the back lot. My reaction fully encompasses how stupid an individual can be. I was such a keener, so I politely declined. I would rather stay and keep rehearsing the dance steps. She looked non-plussed and they went for a walk without me. A couple of my friends, who had overheard her invite me for the walk, launched into me and said, "How dumb are you? Are you for real?" They claimed that they had never seen any greener person in their lives. Looking back, I tend to agree.

Shooting the "Got A Lot Of Livin To Do" (1963) number with Ann-Margret and Bobby Rydell was another blast. All the dance sequences were great fun to do. In one section, Ann-Margret was moving in and out of tables. My friend Pete Menefee, who played Harvey Johnson, and I were at the same table. Ann-Margret came over to us, played with Pete's hair, then came to me and ran her hands over my shoulders. You can sense how lucky we were. I was over the moon.

Ann-Margret, Pete Menefee and James Hibbard in *Bye Bye Birdie,* 1963

When we began to learn Onna White's choreography, we could sense how special this job was going to be. It was inventive, quirky, and fun. We all felt the style was right down our alley. Onna was professional through and through. She was always prepared. Tommy Panko, her assistant choreographer, was a gem to work with. Besides dancing and being featured in the movie, Onna White also chose me, and a dancer named Patty Tribble, to shoot some publicity shots to use for media teasers. She made us feel incredibly special. She was unique. Onna went on to receive an Honorary Academy Award for her choreography of the film *Oliver* (1968). Very few people have received this award. She has also been nominated ten times for Tony awards on Broadway.

Onna White, choreographer, 1963

James Hibbard in publicity still for *Bye Bye Birdie,* 1963

Shooting one segment of the "Telephone Hour" (1963) was a new experience for me. The movie gives the illusion that the actors are on telephone wires dancing, singing, and talking on phones. To achieve this, we were placed on our own platform with a giant blue screen behind us. When we arrived on set, we were all asked if we were scared of heights. I had no fear of heights, so they put me on a platform about twenty-five feet high. This was one of the highest platforms. Everyone else was at various levels. My platform was approximately four feet by four feet square. They used what is called a high-up to raise us up to the level of our platform. For safety, we all had to wear an uncomfortable restrictive harness under our costumes, attached to a wire. The necessity of a safety wire became apparent right away. Onna White's choreography was very energetic, with arms flying and heads bopping back and forth. I found myself twenty-five feet up in the air, with a camera on a crane directly in front of me, and with lights blinding me. It was really hot! We started to rehearse, and everything was going well initially. Suddenly, everything came to a halt. The director, Bob Sidney, yelled, "Cut," and we heard a gasp and a scream. One of the girls had fallen off her platform. She was dangling about a foot down from her perch and the high-up drove in to lift her back up. This continued to happen several times during the shooting of this sequence, even to me. Losing your balance and falling off was terrifying. You have no trust that the wire will hold you until it does. Adrenaline was flying that day. We were all so relieved to finally get the last shot of that sequence, to say the least.

Bye Bye Birdie, 1963

I was lucky enough to be featured in the shower scene sequence of "Telephone Hour" (1963). In the photo below, the girl next to me is Sally Mason. Sally and I were the fortunate ones. Every other dancer in this scene had to sing and dance under shower water. Since we were featured in front, we were nice and dry. We thanked our lucky stars.

James Hibbard and Sally Mason in *Bye Bye Birdie,* 1963

Between the audition and the start of rehearsals, I shot two Heinz Ketchup commercials. It was a unique experience. Sometimes, when you went to an audition for a commercial, you would go in to meet the casting agents and the director and they would have a story board with drawings of the cast and all the separate camera shots they have planned. In this case, when I walked in, their faces looked strange. I turned around to look at what they were looking at and my jaw dropped. Their artists had drawn an exact likeness of me on their story board. You must understand, this is a rare phenomenon. In chorus, they said, "You are the one!" This had never happened before and has only happened only once since this. It was the easiest audition of my life. My one line was kept on the first take, but the rest of the action took many takes. A week later they asked me to come back and do the same commercial again. For my line, it was one take again. They kept the rest of the action from the first shoot in this one. This time the Heinz Ketchup label had both English and French on it, for the Canadian market. This was my first introduction to anything Canadian. It would not be my last.

James Franciscus in *Mr. Novak*, 1963

James Hibbard in Heinz Ketchup commercial, 1959

My agent, Hazel MacMillan, sent me to audition for an acting job on an episode of *Mr. Novak* (1963), a television series starring James Franciscus and Dean Jagger. I got the job. I played a troubled kid in a scene with Mr. Franciscus and a bigger scene with Dean Jagger. Mr. Jagger played the school principal. I played the unruly student, sent to his office for acting up in class. You may remember that Dean Jagger had won a Best Supporting Actor Academy Award for his work in *Twelve o'clock High* (1949), so having a scene with him was a real compliment. He was incredibly supportive and made me feel relaxed.

The next job opportunity was in Las Vegas, doing some choreography for a girl group called The Kim Sisters. One of my mentor/teachers, Dick Humphries, had been choreographing the Kim Sisters for quite a while. He was busy working on another project and recommended that they hire me. His recommendation carried some weight and they agreed. This was to be my first choreographic job. They were a dream to work with. They were an extremely popular lounge act. They were going on tour with Bob Hope's USO

Tour that year and wanted some new staging they could use in their Las Vegas act and on the tour. Those three girls were beautiful. They could sing, dance very well, and play many instruments. They were crazy talented, and they were exciting!

The Kim Sisters, 1962

In November, I auditioned and got a job that would take me back to Las Vegas once more. The Thunderbird Hotel decided to try a new idea. They were going to run two different Broadway musicals each night in their big show lounge. The dinner show was *High Button Shoes* (1947) and the late show was *Anything Goes* (1934). The same cast of artists would be in both shows. The star was Dick Shawn. You will remember his great work in films such as *The Producers* (1967) and *It's A Mad Mad Mad Mad World* (1963). His off the wall comic style served him well in movies, television, and stage work. It was an honour to work with him. I had a featured role in *High Button Shoes* (1947), and I sang and danced in *Anything Goes*

(1934). The set design was ingenious. One side was the dinner show and, it rotated, the other side was *Anything Goes* (1934).

Thunderbird Hotel, Las Vegas, 1964

Patricia Marand and James Hibbard in *High Button Shoes,* 1964

James Hibbard and Dick Shawn in *High Button Shoes,* 1964

Normally, when you went to work in Las Vegas, the rehearsal period was about two or three weeks long and the shows played about the same amount of time. Our shows were unusual because we were setting two entire Broadway musicals. This meant that the rehearsal period was five weeks and we opened December 31, 1962. We ran for six weeks. Dick Shawn left the production after three weeks and was replaced by the original *Hollywood Squares* (1966) host, Peter Marshall. The Thunderbird Hotel made money with the production, but never ventured with this idea again. I loved being in those shows. I have loved being in every show I have ever done. I have been asked, at least a thousand times, what was my favourite show I have ever done. My answer remains the same. Every single one of them, big or small. I have loved every second of it, and I still do.

Chapter Five

Elvis

Promotional posters for Elvis Presley movies, 1964-1967

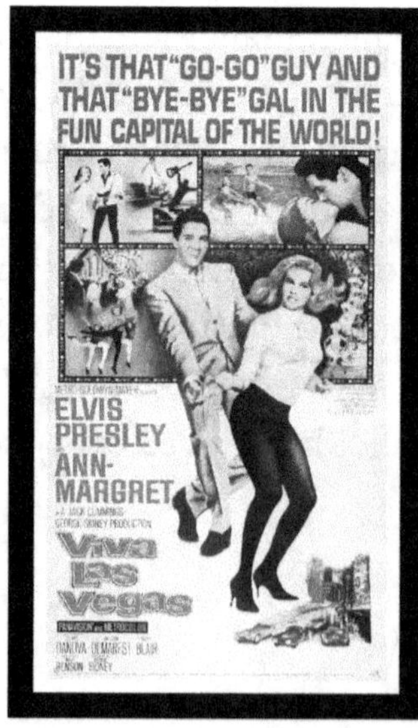

Promotional posters for Elvis Presley movies, 1964-1967

Promotional posters for Elvis Presley movies, 1964-1967

Promotional posters for Elvis Presley movies, 1964-1967

Promotional posters for Elvis Presley movies, 1964-1967

Promotional posters for Elvis Presley movies, 1964-1967

1964 was another full year of work. This year changed my life forever. From roles in the movies *Viva Las Vegas* (1964) and *Kissin*

Cousins (1964), with Elvis Presley, to the stage play *West Side Story* (1957), at the Queen Elizabeth Theatre in Vancouver, BC. This was such a wonderful time. I will save *West Side Story* (1957) for the next chapter, as it really did change my life forever. For now, let me tell you about my experiences with Elvis Presley.

1964 was the year that I danced in my first and second films with Elvis Presley. *Viva Las Vegas* (1964) was filmed during the summer of 1963 and released May 20, 1964. Along with Elvis, it starred the wonderful Ann-Margret and was directed by George Sidney and choreographed by the great David Winters. Ann-Margret, who was David's dance student, recommended that they hire him for the job. This would be David's first time working with Elvis. The film was distributed by MGM.

Kissin Cousins (1964) was also filmed in the summer of 1963 and released on March 6, 1964. It was directed and written by Gene Nelson, my teacher and mentor. Gene Nelson and Gerald Drayson Adams were nominated for a Writers Guild of America Award for screenwriters for the script. The movie was choreographed by Hal Belfer with my friend, Pete Menefee, as assistant choreographer. *Kissin Cousins* (1964) was distributed by MGM. Along with Elvis, the film co-starred Academy Award winners Jack Albertson and Arthur O'Connell.

Just a side note, as it makes for an amusing story. Following every job, everyone in film, television, and theater immediately went to the unemployment office in North Hollywood to file for weekly unemployment checks. Believe me when I say that everyone went. One day, Jack Albertson was standing right next to me in line, and we talked about being in *Kissin Cousins* (1964). While I was waiting in line, I saw a Rolls Royce limo pull up, and out gets none other than Zsa Zsa Gabor. As I said, everyone went there. I can even remember what my unemployment check was. A whopping $65 a week.

Elvis Presley, Jack Albertson, Tommy Farrell and
James Hibbard in *Kissin Cousins,* 1964

During the filming of *Kissin Cousins* (1964), Elvis overheard me talking about my growing up in the woods of Idaho. He asked me to join him at his trailer to have a chat during set up of the next shot. This began our unusual friendship. His entourage, made up of cousins, friends, and his road manager, Joe Esposito, had different responsibilities. One would bring him photos to sign, one took care of his shoes, and the others filled whatever duties he required. Elvis and I would sit at his trailer and talk about hunting and fishing. We talked about our families. He said he did not have much of a chance to talk about normal everyday things anymore. He loved his mom very much and told me how much he missed her. He missed having a normal life. We talked about our early lives, growing up when things were simpler. It made him sad that he could not do anything normal out in public, not even with a disguise. He was constantly mobbed by loving fans. Everything had to be brought to him or he would have to buy out an entire movie theatre, or a restaurant, to have some casual fun with family and friends. Elvis was always so ultra polite. When the assistant director would come and let us know that they were ready for the next shot, Elvis would always say to me, "Jimmy, have we finished our conversation?" and he would always wait for my response. He was always the perfect gentleman. We were simply two buddies talking with each other. We would head back to the where he would become Elvis the King once more.

Jack Albertson, James Hibbard and Elvis Presley in *Kissin Cousins,* 1964

During our conversations, Elvis told me a story about after he had recorded one of his first hit songs. He said he was driving his brand-new Cadillac, with the top down, in Memphis. Some home boys ran up and asked him if he was Elvis Presley. He very proudly said, "Why, yes, I am." One of the boys suddenly punched him in the face and they all ran off. Their girlfriends were in love with Elvis and the boys were jealous. Elvis responded to this by gathering his entourage and learning to defend himself. Some of his cousins, including Red West and Joe Esposito, began taking Karate lessons. Elvis achieved a third-degree black belt level. On the set during some breaks, Red West would demonstrate the prowess Elvis had attained. Red would attack him, and Elvis would beat him into submission. They both were fast as lightning. It was very exciting. Joining him at his trailer continued many times throughout the films we did together. Elvis was a kind, compassionate, generous person. I loved him. We developed a friendship that his road manager, Joe Esposito, told me was something Elvis did not normally do. I was honoured.

I have another memory I would like to share. During breaks on *Kissin' Cousins* (1964), Elvis would bring out his brand-new double neck guitar. He was so proud of it. We had never seen a guitar like it. He would play for us. He was truly gifted, and it was an amazing experience.

I danced in three more films with Elvis. *Girl Happy* (1965) was released March 12, 1965. It was directed by Boris Sagal, choreographed by David Winters, and distributed by MGM. This movie co-starred Shelley Fabares. *Spinout* (1966) was released October 17, 1966. It was directed by Norman Taurog, choreographed by Jack Baker, and distributed by MGM. The movie co-starred Shelley Fabares. *Clambake* (1967) was released October 18, 1967. It was directed by Arthur H. Nadel, choreographed by Alex Romero, and distributed by United Artists. The movie co-starred Shelley Fabares and Bill Bixby, who would go on to become the original Incredible Hulk.

Elvis Presley and James Hibbard in *Spinout,* 1966

The final movie I worked on with Elvis was *Easy Come Easy Go* (1967). It was released March 22, 1967. It was directed by John Rich and distributed by Paramount Pictures. The movie starred Dodie Marshall, Pat Priest and Pat Harrington Jr. Once again David Winters choreographed, but this time I got to assist David in addition to singing and dancing.

Late in the shoot, David had to go to another job, so he asked me to finish for him and stage a picnic production number with Elvis and the rest of cast. It was a fantastic opportunity. We had picnic plates, chairs, tablecloths, and silverware all flying around and set to music. It turned out great and Elvis did everything I asked of him with great ease. After we wrapped, Elvis's Road manager, Joe Esposito, called and invited me to come to the taping of his *68 Comeback TV Special* (1968). Elvis was in fine form, as was his band. I had a VIP front row seat. Elvis and I had a chance to talk after the show and he told me how much he appreciated my work in *Easy Come Easy Go* (1967). He told me that he missed our chats. He was always the gentleman. We had a wonderful time.

James Hibbard in *Easy Come Easy Go,* 1967

Elvis Presley and James Hibbard,
2021 in *Easy Come Easy Go*, 1967

I do not take lightly all of the great times I had working with Elvis Presley. He was a consummate professional. He always knew his lines and was generous as an actor. For a unique moment in my life, we were also friends.

Chapter Six

Meeting The Love Of My Life

Charlene Brandolini and James Hibbard, 2021

I heard through the grapevine about an audition for *West Side Story* (1957) that was to be produced in Seattle, Washington and Vancouver, Canada. It was to be put together by the Vancouver International Festival. The festival was a huge yearly summer event. They brought in many Broadway shows, some with the original stars. Several of my friends, including Walter Painter and Anita Mann, went to the audition being held in Los Angeles.

At the audition, I met Gus Trikonis, Suzy Kaye, and Bobby Thompson. They had all performed in the 1961 movie and Broadway versions of *West Side Story* (1957). I also met Lou Procopio, who was destined to play the role of Bernardo, leader of the Sharks.

One of the people involved in putting the production together was Hugh Pickett, a prominent impressario in Canada. He handled all the publicity. His company was Famous Artist Ltd. They had an office based in Seattle and another in Vancouver. Hugh Pickett became a very important figure in my life. The director/choreographer was Aida Broadbent, well known in Los Angeles for choreographing the *Jimmy Durante Show* (1954) and various Los Angeles Civic Light Opera productions.

My dance friends Walter Painter, Anita Mann, and I were hired for the job. We soon met some new friends, including Gus Trikonis, Suzy Kaye, Bobby Thompson, and Lou Procopio. I was cast as Arab, Walter was cast as Action, Anita was Anybodys, Lou Procopio was Bernardo, leader of the Sharks, Bobby was Snowboy, Gus Trikonis was Riff, leader of the Jets, and Suzy Kaye was Anita. An interesting turn of events happened. Bobby Thompson became the choreographer of this production. He, Gus Trikonis and Suzy Kaye had been in the Broadway production and the 1961 movie of *West Side Story* (1957), and they knew all the original Jerome Robbins choreography. It was important because, at that time, any production of *West Side Story* (1957) was required to use Jerome Robbins's choreography. You could not stage it with new dance work. Aida Broadbent, for the integrity of the production, remained the director and graciously stepped aside to allow Bobby to perform the choreographic duties. Bobby's assistants were naturally Gus Trikonis and Suzy Kaye. What a profound blessing this was for us to do the original dances. Although the dances were extremely difficult to do, they were extremely rewarding. Jerome Robbins's dance work was technically an entirely different level to achieve. When you can do his choreography correctly, you truly became of age as a dancer.

Suzy Kaye and James Hibbard in *West Side Story,* 1964

When we arrived in Vancouver and drove across the Granville Street bridge, I instantly fell in love with the city. The air was crisp and the smells from the lumber mills below the bridge wafted up, which reminded me of Idaho. I immediately thought that Vancouver was a beautiful city.

Granville Street Bridge, 1964

Queen Elizabeth Theatre, 1964

On the first day of rehearsal at the Queen Elizabeth Theatre, we met with the producer, director, choreographer, costume designer, set designer, and the rest of the cast. We knew right away we were in good hands. Our stars were Marlys Waters and Don McKay, the original London leads, as Tony and Maria. Our conductor was Lawrence Foster, who was on loan to us from the San Francisco Ballet Company. What a bonus! The dancers cast from Vancouver included Vicki LaBelle, Rosanne Hopkins, Diane Farris, Karen Fawcett, and Vicky Armstrong. They were all fantastic. They were all good singers and dancers. The atmosphere was electric. We were all taken on a tour of the theatre complex. Some of us had never been on a stage that big. We felt so small, looking out at the empty two thousand and eight hundred seat house. It was an awesome sight!

Bobby Thompson, Gus Trikonis, and Suzy Kaye staged all the original Jerome Robbins choreography. On Broadway, and in the movie, Jerome Robbins required that the Jets and the Sharks not mingle at all. This kept it authentic, just as it was in the movie and the Broadway production. We did the same. It was impressive. We played tricks on the Sharks, such as raiding their dressings rooms. We sprayed awful cologne on their costumes. The Sharks did the same to us. As Jets we wore our colours all the time, and we stuck together on breaks. When we went out to lunch we stayed close together, as a gang would do. We made people on the streets of Vancouver go around us, and we would glare and laugh at them. It all worked. It was great fun, promotional stuff. The atmosphere was set, and the mystique was created.

James Hibbard rehearsing *West Side Story*, 1964

James Hibbard rehearsing *West Side Story*, 1964

James Hibbard rehearsing *West Side Story*, 1964

James Hibbard rehearsing *West Side Story*, 1964

On the second day of rehearsal an amazing thing happened. The girl signed to play one of the Sharks, Rosalia, arrived fresh off the plane from performing in a musical revue in Montreal, Quebec. Before she could take off her coat the director, Aida Broadbent, instructed her to sing *Somewhere* (1957) for us. Most artists would demand to take time to warm up prior to singing such a demanding song. This girl, being the trooper she was, just rolled with it. I could not take my eyes off her, and neither could anyone else. Our great musical conductor, Lawrence Foster, sat down at the piano and this girl began to sing. When she finished, the room was eerily silent, before erupting with applause and cheers. She was stunning. All of us seasoned Los Angeles professionals felt blown away. I fell in love with her at first sight. Right then and there I decided that I was going to marry this girl. This young country boy from Idaho was smitten. As she was walking across the floor, I went up to her in a stupor and said something goofy, "You sing real good." The girl's name was Charlene Brandolini.

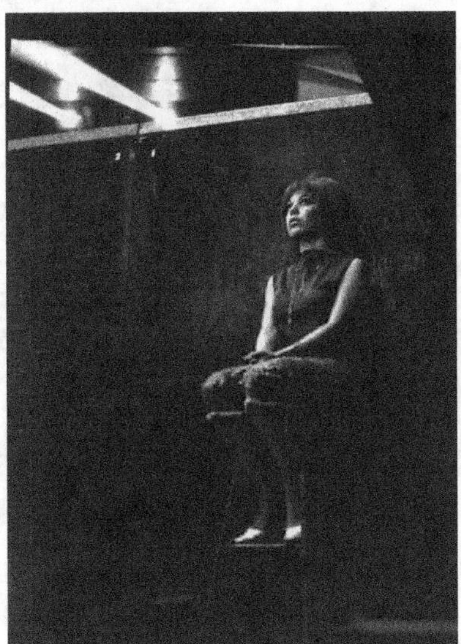

Charlene Brandolini in the orchestra pit of the Queen Elizabeth Theatre, 1964

All of the cast had the feeling that we had a great show. We rehearsed for three weeks, during which time I dated Charlene. We opened in Seattle, at the Seattle Civic Theatre, for a one week run. Then we returned to Vancouver for our two-week run at the Queen Elizabeth Theatre. Our reviews were, across the board, raves. We still hold the record for attendance at the Queen Elizabeth Theatre for a two-week run. It was rare for a theatre run to have everything work as it was supposed to. Everything just clicked into place. There was not a weak spot in the whole production. Plus, we all had the great flattering pleasure of getting seven to eleven curtain calls per performance. The Broadway phenomenon happened for us, too. At the end of the show, there was silence, followed by one or two people clapping slowly. Then the audience jumped out of their chairs and just exploded with applause and cheers. Most of us had never experienced this before. During this production, my life changed forever, and all for the better.

James Hibbard, David Nage, and Anita Mann in *West Side Story*, 1964

One or two nights before closing the show, I proposed to Miss Charlene Brandolini. Yes, the same girl I had met just six weeks ago in the rehearsal hall of the Queen Elizabeth Theatre. To my great luck, she said accepted. Oh my God! I knew from the moment I met her that this was the girl for me. My angels have always looked out for me, but now they were working overtime.

Charlene and I made our plans to marry on October 15, 1964. I returned to Los Angeles, and we got to know each other better through phone calls and letters. I had three projects to do before getting married. I had signed with KTLA Studios to choreograph three television specials in a row. The first one starred teen idol, Frankie Avalon, who was a huge star. He also flirted with all the girls constantly. After filming his special, he called and asked if I was interested in choreographing his new act for touring. I said that I was, of course. I joined him at his home one night and went over his structure for the show. I liked it. He wanted to have four girls in the act and start rehearsals right away. The only snag was that he wanted me to stage his entire show for free and convince all four girls to do the same. He said it would be great exposure and it should be an honour to collaborate with him. I was polite and told him I had already paid my dues and people can die from exposure. He was upset, but I wished him well and left with my head held high. The new act never materialized. The second special starred Broadway star Jack Cassidy, who was married to movie star, Shirley Jones. Jack Cassidy was friendly, professional to the core, and brilliantly talented. He was one classy dude. He was gracious and complimentary to all of us. The last special was with the one and only Mickey Rooney. Mickey was a force of nature. He was difficult to work with. Each time we were ready to shoot a segment, the assistant director had to find Mickey. He would be in his dressing room on the phone betting on the horses with his bookie, or so the assistant director told me. While on the set he was the powerhouse performer he had always been known for. We were not always sure of exactly what he was going to do, but he was funny and explosive. I do not remember him speaking very much to me at all. It was crazy. I had six dancers on each show. It was a wonderful experience working with each of these legends, and a great learning curve.

My mind, however, was consumed with my upcoming marriage to Charlene.

James Hibbard and Charlene Brandolini, 1964

Charlene's and my romance was a whirlwind of note. From meeting her in the rehearsal hall in the Queen Elizabeth Theatre to my proposing and her accepting took all of six weeks. From that wild and wonderful summer in Vancouver, Charlene and I were apart until September. At that point, we travelled to Idaho. I wanted my parents to meet her. Growing up in Idaho, my family always enjoyed holidays by getting together and camping in the woods near a lake or river. Everyone had their tents, and my parents had a big Winnebago RV. I was in my element, but Charlene was not. Charlene was a city girl through and through. I have to hand it to her, she made the best of it. I know now that the mosquitos, the outdoor toilets, my going fishing for hours, and the animal sounds each night were more than she bargained for. To my great good fortune, that experience did not change her mind.

Charlene's heritage was Italian. Her mom, Ermie, had family from the south of Italy and her dad, Gillie, had family from Northern Italy. They were absolutely stunned with the news of our engagement, as were the rest of her family. My family, who travelled from Boise, Idaho for the wedding, included my mother, Lois, my dad, Mike, my brother, Frosty, who was my best man, and his wife, Shannon, and their kids. All of Charlene's family were there. Her mom and dad, her Aunty Elma, her brothers, Leon and Harry, and many aunts, uncles, and cousins.

I talked earlier about Hugh Pickett, the Entrepreneur who brought me to Vancouver to perform in *West Side Story* (1957). He was best lifetime friends with Charlene. His company was Famous Artists Ltd. Hugh's partner ran the head office in Seattle and Hugh ran the branch office in Vancouver. He was responsible not only for the publicity of *West Side Story* (1957), but his company also brought in international stars to Vancouver, such as Marlene Dietrich, Rudolf Nureyev, Leontyne Price, and Elvis Presley. He produced many shows for Theatre Under the Stars when it was entirely professional. Charlene featured in many of those productions. Hugh, Charlene, and I have remained best of friends throughout our lives. He graciously provided Charlene's stunning wedding dress and veil. As an extra wedding present, he gave us our wedding night at the very upscale Bayshore Hotel. Hugh was a wonderful man. He was very generous and giving. He was also a highly respected theatre critic. He wrote reviews for the Vancouver Sun and the West Ender publications. No matter who you were, he was honest to the core, and he was the voice of Vancouver theatre for many years. Some of the best reviews Charlene and I have had were from Hugh Pickett. Most importantly he was our friend. We miss him every day.

James Hibbard and Charlene Brandolini and the wedding party, 1964

Hugh Pickett

Charlene and I were married in Vancouver, BC, on October 15, 1964. The ceremony was at the Saint Peter and Paul Catholic Church and was officiated by Father Swinkles, who also married Pierre Trudeau, father of Justin Trudeau. Our wedding reception was held at the Marine Golf Club. It seemed to me that the entire

Italian community of Vancouver was there. It was spectacular. Two days after our wedding, we were on our way to Los Angeles and my family were on their way back to Idaho. Charlene's wonderful family were in visible shock as we drove away from her home, heading for West Hollywood. I can still see, in my mind's eye, her parents staring at us as we went down Granville Street, watching until we were out of sight. We had a wonderful trip to Los Angeles. We took the coastal route, and it was a beautiful drive. I had the woman of my dreams. Life could not get better than this.

Valley Music Theater, Woodland Hills, Calif. 1964

Cast of *West Side Story*, Valley Music Theatre, 1964

I had my bride, and I was in seventh heaven. Charlene and I got our first apartment on North Sweetzer Avenue in the heart of West Hollywood. After two months, another apartment came available across the street, and we moved. The owners were Abe and Molly, two lovely people. We became great friends. They owned a small coffee shop on the corner of Sweetzer Avenue and Santa Monica Boulevard. We ate there on a regular basis. During this time, I was performing in another production of *West Side Story* (1957) at the Valley Music Theatre in San Fernando Valley. I played Arab again and my best friend, Walter Painter, played Action. Anita Mann reprised her role of Anybodys, and Bobby Thompson played Snowboy once again. Also in the cast was the great Teri Garr. Terri played Velma, one of the Jets. The leads in this production were Carla's sister is Anna Marie Alberghetti. She played Maria. Brian Avery played opposite her as Tony. At this time, the Theatre in the Round concept was an experiment created by theatre arts students in Southern California. It held 2865 seats, which was huge by any standard. Several other venues also tried it throughout Southern California.

A very funny thing happened during the run at the Valley Music Theatre. Carla Alberghetti wore a Vega mic during the show. One night, at intermission, the sound engineers forgot to turn off Ms. Alberghetti's microphone. Everything that she said and did was broadcast to the audience and into our dressing rooms. This included her time in the bathroom. I mean, we heard everything. One of the girls raced to Carla's dressing room to alert her, but it was too late. The audience and everyone backstage had heard plenty. When act two started we were still laughing, and the audience was in a state of shock. Carla was such a lovely woman. We felt so badly for her. She was so embarrassed and furious with the sound guys when she was told why the audience was laughing during the inter-mission. When I think about it today, it still makes me laugh. Sorry, Carla.

Charlene was signed to perform in *West Side Story* for a Theatre In The Round circuit, which included Anaheim, and San Carlos. She reprised her role of Rosalia and sang *Somewhere* (1957). The star of this tour was the popular singing sensation, Pat Boone. Pat Boone was an absolute gentleman. I finished my run at the Valley Music Theatre and Charlene continued her tour with Pat Boone. We became good friends with Pat and his family during the tour. He had a lovely family that included his wife Shirley and their four daughters. One of their daughters, Debby Boone, had the hit record *You Light Up My Life* (1977).

Soon, a spectacular two-bedroom apartment on North Sweetzer Avenue became available. It was located just north of Melrose Avenue, at 736 North Sweetzer Avenue. We needed a place with more room because we were planning on starting a family. There were four apartments in the building. Our rent was $115 per month. These days, each of the apartments sell for more than three million dollars each. We were living smack dab in the middle of West Hollywood. Life was great. We became great friends with our neighbours, Nat and Ina Cohn. Ina had just given birth to their second daughter, Mindy. Our daughter, Gianna, and Mindy were the same age and had a lot of play dates. Mindy later became an actress on *The Facts of Life* (1979), a hugely popular television series, and was the voice of Velma for many years on the television series *Scooby-Doo* (1969). Such a small world. This area of West Hollywood was a melting pot for all artists in the business.

At the corner of Sweetzer Avenue and Santa Monica Boulevard was a market called the Arrow Market. We shopped there all the time, and we would regularly see Sonny and Cher, Sal Mineo, or Billy Gray shopping for dinner and groceries. This area in West Hollywood is still an artist haven, but now it has become a high rent district. The building we lived in, and the building next door have not changed one little bit. Charlene and I finished the year off working in two different productions of *West Side Story* (1957) for

Theater In The Round, and just like that 1964 was over. A momentous year, to say the least.

From January to February 1965 there was a break in work, and it gave me an excellent opportunity to get back into class. I took jazz classes, with Toni Basil and David Winters, at the Coronet Theater on La Cienega Boulevard. I packed in as much as I could. It was an ideal time to get my chops back and get ready for whatever was to come. And, boy, did it ever come. Early in February, 1965, Toni Basil hired me to be her assistant choreographer and dance on a pilot for Dick Clark's television series *Where The Action Is* (1965). It was such an exciting time.

Chapter Seven

Dick Clarke *Where The Action Is*

Where The Action Is logo, 1965

The pilot for *Where The Action Is* (1965) was shot in February, 1965. Half of the pilot was shot on the beach at Malibu, and half of the pilot was shot in the mountains at Big Bear. Only one portion was from Philadelphia, for Bobby Rydell's segment. It was choreographed by the renowned Toni Basil. I was her assistant choreographer on this project. Toni Basil was a singer, songwriter, film maker, film director, dancer, visionary, and recording star. She was solely responsible for bringing street dancing mainstream. She and Don Campbell formed the dancing crew, the Campbellockers, the pioneers of street dancing.

The stars of this show were Paul Revere and the Raiders, The Supremes, Frankie Avalon, Bobby Rydell, The Four Seasons, Bobby Freeman, Chad and Jeremy, Jan and Dean, Jackie and Gayle, and Dick and Dee Dee. Toni Basil and I, along with the rest of the dancers, rode on a touring bus up to Big Bear. To entertain ourselves we sang and danced the entire way. From my experience, dancers love to dance to the songs and interpret the lyrics as much as possible.

The Supremes sang *Stop in the Name of Love* (1965) and I genu-inely believe the signature move The Supremes used in that song, of pushing their hand forward in the stop motion, was created by them and the dancers on that bus ride. It certainly was a logical move. All the way to Big Bear each of the stars sang their hits and we all sang and danced along. It was one of the most enjoyable bus rides I have ever had.

In Malibu, we had our introduction to dancing in the sand. While it was tough enough to do all these dance styles in a dance studio, doing them in sand was a different story. We persevered and eventually got it down. Our guest stars on the beach portion were Jan and Dean, Bobby Freeman, Dick and Dee Dee, Jackie and Gayle, our hosts, Linda Scott and Steve Alaimo.

When we finished shooting the pilot, we waited for weeks with bated breath to hear the outcome. What a thrill it was to get the news that ABC bought it and we were going to do the series. Toni Basil did a great job of choreographing the pilot. Dick Clark asked her to continue as choreographer of the series. This was where Toni Basil changed my professional life forever. As I recall, she had other work lined up to do and asked Dick Clark Productions to hire me as choreographer. Toni Basil was a bright light in the industry as a singer, dancer, actress, choreographer, director, producer, and photographer. She had always been ahead of the times, and a true visionary. We are still good friends and her kindness and generos-ity helped propel me in my career at the right time. Thanks to her, Dick Clark did hire me to choreograph the first season of *Where the Action Is* (1965). In one moment, she helped establish me as one of the working choreographers in the business. I owe so much to Toni. I love her dearly and admire her. Her smash hit record *Mickey* (1982) was the first record video ever. She was the one person cred-ited for bringing street dancing, locking, popping, break dancing, and vibration to the mainstream. Toni was a major force and still a fierce dancer. Her YouTube Channel Toni Basil's House is amazing.

Most recently, Toni choreographed Quentin Tarrantino's film *Once Upon A Time In Hollywood* (2019), recreating the dance styles from the 60s. They could not have chosen a better person to do this. She was, and still is, The Bomb.

Toni Basil, choreographer

In 1965, *Where The Action Is* (1965) was created and produced by Dick Clark Productions. It premiered on June 27, 1965, and ran until March 31, 1967. The theme song for the show, *Action* (1964), was recorded by Freddy Cannon. The song peaked on the charts at number thirteen in September, 1965. This show was a spinoff of *American Bandstand* (1952). Dick Clark had a brief cameo in the pilot episode, but after that he only did voice overs to introduce the performers. The initial season was directed by Hal Galli, and I was the choreographer. My assistant choreographer was Lesley Evans, who was also one of the Action Kids.

Each episode had hit recording artists who were topping the charts performing each week. We had our regular cast of stars, such as Paul Revere and the Raiders as our house band, and Linda Scott and Steve Alaimo, who hosted and sang hit songs. Our group of dancers were Pete Menefee, Lesley Evans, Joy Ciro, Jeri Lynn Stapleton, Jill Gordon, Roberta Tennes, Cathy Anderson, Roger Minami, Michael Schwartz, and yours truly. We became known as the Action Kids. Pete Menefee and I were the oldest kids. Pete was twenty-two and I was twenty-one. All the shows in the initial season were in black and white, filmed at various locations in Southern California and once in Hawaii.

As a side note, when you talk about six degrees of separation, this is crazy. Paul Revere and the Raiders was our house band. I was a fan of them long before I met them. It turned out that Paul and I were from the same hometown in Boise, Idaho. Paul moved to Caldwell, Idaho, twenty-seven and a half miles from Boise. We were only twenty-seven minutes from each other, yet we did not meet until we ended up working together on the same television series pilot eight years later in Hollywood. This is serendipitous. Who would have thought it. This kind of coincidence is amazing, and it still gives me a thrill thinking about it.

Paul Revere and The Raiders, 1965

Paul Revere and The Raiders, 1965

With my new duties as choreographer of season one, I had the responsibility of auditioning and choosing who would be our regular dancers. I chose some of the dancers who worked with us on the pilot, but also some new ones. The dance studio in North Hollywood at Vine Street and Yucca was called the Cherokee Studios. It was packed with *Where The Action Is* (1965) hopefuls. The choices I made were quite easy. The dancers who made the show were the cream of the crop. Not only were they professional dancers who could dance all the current styles, they were the right age, beautiful and were full of vibrant personality. We were all on our way.

On the first day of rehearsal, there was palpable electricity in the air. Dick Clark sent me about twenty songs by various recording artists who were to guest star on the show. All I knew were the possible locations each artist would perform. It could be at a beach, or an amusement park, or anywhere. If you are rehearsing in a studio and then shooting in a studio, you know exactly what to expect from the director. This was all unknown.

After about a week or so of rehearsing in the studio for the first episode, we were off to location after location. We would arrive at a chosen location and the director, Hal Galli, would quickly choose where he wanted to shoot the number. Sometimes Hal would suddenly say, "I don't like it here. I'd like to shoot this number on the rock outcropping over there." Since this was uneven ground, the choreography I had set in the studio would not work on the pile of rocks he had chosen. I knew at that instant that I had to be ready for these changes and adapt my choreography accordingly. The bright side of this was that I learned not to get excited, to stay calm, and to adapt and quickly change the staging to work in any location. You can not get frantic and must just take a breath and work quickly. It was spectacular training. Fortunately, I had the best group of dancers to do this. They were able to adapt to anything that was required of them. For me, this newly acquired skill has served me very well throughout my entire professional career.

Steve Alaimo and The Action Kids in *Where The Action Is*, 1965

The other skill I developed was to choreograph and then dance in the numbers myself. It was usual to choreograph a routine and not dance in the number. That way, you get to concentrate on the energy, spacing, camera angles, and overall performance levels. When you choreograph and dance in the number you have to switch off choreographer mode and become the performer. Then you can just worry about your own spacing and execution of the dance. Gradually, it became less of a stressful process. It was a harrowing learning curve, but it has served me well.

Pete Menefee, Roger Minami, James Hibbard and
Michael Schwartz at Malibu Beach, 1965

One day, the guest star was the great James Brown. Throughout the first season, James Brown would guest star on many episodes. We all did our best to dance like him in the rehearsal studio. His fast foot twizzles from side to side were a signature move of his own creation. I particularly enjoyed perfecting this move. He appreciated my imitation of him. After every show, he would give all of us a gift. One time he gave us jewellery. All were oversized baubles, of different shapes, in the form of bracelets, necklaces, and earrings. We called them clunky. Today, that kind of jewellery is in style. I did not appreciate it as much back then as I would today. I wish I still had his gifts. I gave them to my dancing girls or fans in the crowd. He was always so friendly, professional, and kind. We loved dancing behind him and his band.

One of the new experiences most of us had never encountered was having fans. The fan base just grew and grew. Fan letters began to pour in. All of us had our own group of fans. It was certainly a new thrill, and we loved every moment of it. We always had an audience, no matter where we went. It sure helped to have their energy. The thrill of performing live is like no other. Today, on Facebook, there is a tribute page for Fans of the Action Kids. It is comprised of fans of the show and created by fan, and now friend, Richard Norcutt.

We filmed in many great locations. One time we did an entire episode on Olvera Street, known as the Birthplace of Los Angeles. It was the original street in Los Angeles and, of course, its history is Mexican. It is a must-see area for any tourist in California. We had a great time there. If memory serves, one of our guest stars this day was the female singing group, Martha and the Vandellas. They sang two of their hits *Dancing in the Street* (1965) and *Nowhere to Run* (1965). We were also lucky enough to be treated to a fantastic trip to Hawaii.

Where The Action Is, 1965

Where The Action Is, Hawaii, 1965

The Action Kids, Hawaii, 1965

On the first day of filming in Hawaii, six of us boys each had one of the letters spelling A C T I O N painted in black on our bare chests. After we had washed off the letter, you could still see it clearly on our chests. This was because shooting in the hot sun got us all sunburned, and the letters showed up like white paint against our red skin. Ouch. It was too bad we did not have cell phones back then. Those photos would have been hysterical. My skin was very pale, so for the remainder of our time in Hawaii I remained covered. The fans at every location in Hawaii were fantastic. They helped make our time there a wonderful experience.

Filming *Where The Action Is*, Hawaii, 1965

After the first season was over, I left the show to pursue other ventures. The concept of Where *The Action Is* (1965) was one of television lore. It was an *American Bandstand* (1952) spinoff created by Dick Clark. Back then there were no videos. For the first time you got to see your favourite recording artists performing their hit songs every day, Monday through Friday. Some of the artists who graced the show were The Beach Boys, Sonny and Cher, The Righteous Brothers, James Brown, Chad and Jeremy, Diana Ross and The Supremes, Jackie DeShannon, Frankie Avalon, Bobby Rydell,

Bobby Freeman, The Byrds, The Mamas and the Papas, The Shirelles, The Four Seasons, Donovan, Martha and the Vandellas, The Animals, and Freddy Cannon. *Where The Action Is* (1965) has furthered all our careers. There was not a recording artist who did not want to be on the show. We all owe a great debt of gratitude to Dick Clark and his vision.

A few years after I left the show, I happened to run into Dick Clark at the Los Angeles airport. We had become good friends during the first season on the show. We reminisced for quite a while about the series. He was very complimentary of my work. Before we parted, he said, "Always carry your wardrobe bag with the hanger tips facing outward so you won't scratch your face." Dick Clark was a gentleman.

Dick Clark, 1965

The Action Kids

Pete Menefee, 1962

Pete Menefee was a superb dancer and had many movie, television, and stage credits in his resume. In 1972, he quit dancing to pursue his dream of becoming a costume designer. He has been spectacularly successful as a costume designer, winning three Prime Time TV Emmy Awards. His costume design work has taken him worldwide. He is now happily retired and living in one of the most beautiful homes in the Hollywood Hills. He also created his stunning garden. We are still the best of friends. We communicate all the time on Facebook and whenever I am in Los Angeles, we always get together.

Joy Ciro, 1964

Joy Ciro and Bobby Hatfield, of the Righteous Brothers, met on *Where The Action Is* (1965) and they married. Bobby passed away in 2003 and Joy passed away in 2014.

Lesley Evans, 1966

Lesley Evans lives in her beautiful home in Bel Aire, near Beverly Hills. We are in constant touch and see each other every time I am in Los Angeles. Lesley was the first person to encourage me to write my memoirs.

Michael Schwartz, 1964

Michael Schwartz lives in Mar Vista, West Los Angeles, and has a beautiful family. He is still acting. He founded an organization called One On One Outreach. They provide food and necessities to people in need throughout the year. Mike also teaches the Meisner method of acting at the Ruskin School in Southern California. I hope to see him next time I am in town.

Jeri Lynn Stapleton, 1965

Jeri Lynn Stapleton has been an advocate for women's rights ever since being an Action Kid. She is currently President of California Now, which is a National Organization for Women. She is a force.

Jill Gordon, 1965

Jill Gordon is still dancing. She was recently featured on a video with Miley Cyrus. She also keeps her chops up by taking tap and jazz classes every week. She is thumping and bumping. Jill is healthy and happy, living in Los Angles with her family. I get to see her each time I am there.

Roberta Tennes, 1965

Roberta Tennes danced in two Elvis Presley films, *Red Line 7000* (1965) and *Clambake* (9167). I am sorry to say that I lost touch with her. She was such a beautiful person, inside and out. Roberta passed away many years ago.

Cathy Andreason, 1965

Cathy Anderson – I am sorry to say I have lost touch with her.

Roger Minami, 1965

Roger Minami is currently retired but, after *Where The Action Is* (1965), he designed and built homes from Canada to Mexico. He also designed sets, lights, and costumes, and choreographed various nightclub shows in Las Vegas, Reno, and Lake Tahoe. He still loves dancing. He keeps in shape by taking Zumba classes every week. He lives in Mexico.

James Hibbard, 1965

James Hibbard is still choreographing, directing, dancing, acting, and singing in movies, television, and on stage. I teach tap at many dance studios in Vancouver, British Columbia. I have taught at Harbour Dance Centre for thirty-seven years. I am also on the faculty at Capilano University, where I teach tap and jazz to theatre arts students. I live in North Vancouver, British Columbia, Canada with my beautiful family.

Paul Revere and The Raiders and The Action Kids, 1965

Chapter Eight

Friends and Stars

I would like to take the time here to mention the many friends and stars I have worked with over the years. These people were all so incredibly special to me. There are so many people I must honour in my life and career in show business. It is almost countless, but here goes.

Susan Skemp

Susan Skemp - Singer, Actor, Writer, Director, Producer

Susan is a singer, actor, writer, director, producer. She co-starred in two stage productions I choreographed. One was Godspell at the Vancouver Playhouse and the other was Anything Goes at the Stanley Park outdoor theatre, Theatre Under the Stars at Malkin Bowl.

For the last 7 years she has been my tight hand 'girl Friday' with all things related to getting my book prepared for publishing. Her personality is super positive, which has proven to be worth it's weight in gold.

She has helped me edit my story. She has done all the researching necessary, and has supported me all along the way without flinching. Frankly, I wouldn't be where I am with my story without her assistance.

Pam Rosa (nee Quick)

Pam Rosa - Dancer, Singer, Actor, Choreographer, Studio Owner

Pam is one of my best friends. She is also an outstanding dancer who has worked for me in most of the TV and stage productions I have Choreographed and Directed. My dancers at the Canadian Broadcasting System (CBC) were billed as Jame's Angels. Pam is one of my Jame's Angels. She is also part owner of one of the most successful dance studios in Canada, the Harbour Dance Centre. I've been teaching tap and Jazz for her for more than 30 years. I love her dearly.

Jennifer Bishop

Jennifer Bishop - Dancer, Singer, Actor, Choreographer, Studio Owner

Jennifer is an accomplished dancer/singer. I adjudicated her as a young girl in a dance festival and she still has my remarks about her dancing in her drawer at home. Jennifer owns her own dance studio, The Rhythm Room, and I've taught tap for her for more than 20 years. We are the best of friends.

Jennifer founded the West Coast Tap Collective. In 2004 they presented me with a Lifetime Achievement Award and in the same year she was instrumental in getting the BC Entertainment Hall of Fame to award me with my star, which is embedded in the sidewalk in front of the world famous Orpheum Theatre, similar to the Hollywood Boulevard Walk of Fame.

She is another angel in my life.

Pete Menefee

Pete Menefee- Dancer/ Costume Designer

Pete was one of my best friends. We danced together in many of the same films and television shows in the 60s and 70s. Each time I go to Los Angeles for the Professional Dancers Society Gypsy Awards event, we get together for lunch or dinner and reminisce royally. Pete was a multi-talented, thoroughly charming, dignified dude. He has a beautiful home in the Hollywood Hills and his garden is a work of art.

Pete was one year my senior, which I will not let him forget. He was such a good dancer. His style was quirky, so he was recognizable in every production. He was well trained and could turn like a top. He was also an excellent tap dancer. We met in the movie *Bye Bye Birdie* (1963). Pete was a featured actor. He played Harvey Johnson and was very funny. Pete's contract was under Screen Actors Guild, and he still gets residuals every time the movie runs. My contract was under Screen Extras Guild, so I do not get any residuals from that film.

In 1965, I was hired to choreograph *Where the Action Is* (1965). Pete Menefee was my first choice to become one of the Action Kid dancers on the show. In all we had ten dancers, including myself. Pete quickly became a fan favourite. Everyone loved him. We all started to receive fan mail, which was new to all of us. After I left the show, Pete remained in the series until it ran its course in 1967.

Pete and I danced in several Elvis Presley films and in Nancy Sinatra's television special *Movin' With Nancy* (1967). We did two other projects with Ann-Margret, her first nightclub act in Las Vegas and her CBS television special *From Hollywood With Love* (1969). The last job we danced together in was the film *The One And Only Genuine Original Family Band* (1968) at Walt Disney Studios.

In one major scene, two political parties at a convention break out into a food fight brawl. Both Pete and I got a bump up in pay because it required some stunt work, and we were up to that challenge. This was great. The different food and drink were flying everywhere, and we were soon covered with it. Because of the hot lights and long shoot, the aroma from the food turned very sour and dancers began gagging. Boy, did we smell bad! To keep all the shots matching we were not able to take the splattered food off our faces and clothes, even when we went on breaks and for lunch. It was extremely uncomfortable, but it was a barrel of fun.

Shortly after this film, I moved to Canada. Pete decided to retire from dancing and fulfill his dream of becoming a costume designer.

He became one of the most successful costume designers in the business. He has won 5 Prime Time Emmys for his costume design for television. Most importantly, Pete Menefee and I are still the best of friends. Every year that I can go to Los Angeles, Pete and I always meet up and spend some time reminiscing and getting caught up with each others lives. Dancer camaraderie is long lasting and true to the bone. Every time we get together, even though so much time has passed, it is though no time has passed at all. You just pick up there you left off thirty-five plus years ago, and you continue your conversation. It is always a profound experience for me.

Milo O'Shea

Milo O'Shea- Actor

Milo O'Shea was an Irish actor with an extensive career in film, television, and stage. He was nominated twice for Tony Awards on Broadway. I do not remember the exact year, but it was between 1962 and 1964. I was cast in a new musical play to be mounted at the San Bernardino Civic Light Opera Theater. The star was Milo O'Shea. I think it was the first show Milo did after coming from Ireland. Mr. O'Shea was very gracious. The Director/Writer/Choreographer was Jack Bunch, who choreographed many movies and television episodes. It was at Jack Bunch's prodding that Milo came to America. Jack was working in Europe and discovered Milo O'Shea. The rest is show business history. Milo O'Shea's career took off and he became a prolific star of stage, screen, and television.

Bert Michaels

Bert Michaels- Actor/Dancer

I have two friends I want to tell you about, Bert Michaels and Irwin Berniker. I met and worked with both in the movie *Gypsy* (1962). Our experiences were intertwined, so it is easier to share them together with you.

After I finished filming *Gypsy* (1962), my new friend, Irwin Berniker, and I were inseparable. We used to hunt Jack rabbits way out in the San Fernando Valley. He also taught me how to play snooker. Snooker is a table game like pool, only the table is bigger, and the balls are smaller. It requires great precision to play it well. Irwin took me to a pool hall on Santa Monica Boulevard, in West Hollywood, called Mothers. Irwin and I spent a lot of time in this pool hall. We would play each other for small change. I discovered that I was good at this game, which led me to playing other people for table time or even more money. I became good enough to make enough money to augment my income from my dancing jobs.

Mothers was a pool hall right out of movies like *The Hustler* (1962). It was seedy and dark and had three pool tables, three snooker tables, and a small café. Sometimes, on Saturdays and Sundays, I would even go there for breakfast before starting to play. There were players there who were professional. They played for serious money. It was not unusual to see games played for $500 to $1000 a game. This was out of my league. These players had names like Harry the Hat, or Nick the Slip. They were names you might recognise from Abe Burrows *Guys and Dolls* (1955). One night, we were watching a game and the prize was $1,500. It was best out of three. This was serious. After the game, the loser did not have enough money to pay up. The winner, and two of his buddies, dragged the guy out back to the lane and promptly broke his thumbs. These guys did not fool around. This was a clear sign to me that my attraction to playing for money was not the direction I should go. I quit playing for money right away.

One night, Irwin and I were bored. He said, "Let's have an adventure." He told me there was a house he knew of in the Hollywood Hills. He said there was never anyone there and you could easily climb up the outside wall and look in, and even go for a swim in the pool. This sounded good to me because I was young and stupid. The house was stunning. It looked like a mausoleum in an Arabian desert. The house was designed by Frank Lloyd Wright and was magnificent to see. The outside wall was tiered so you could climb it with ease. Irwin's girlfriend, Paula, accompanied us. We started to climb, but the wall was so tall it took a while to get to the top. I reached the top of the wall, with Paula right below me and Irwin to my left, and looked into a beautiful courtyard. The house was made of stone and had a gorgeous, inviting swimming pool. Irwin told me he had done this before which, as I think about it now, I should have been sceptical about. He said, "Let's go for a swim." It was a hot summer night, so this sounded great to me. I started to climb over the wall and looked back at Paula below me. Everything was quiet and looked good. I looked back at the house and, out of nowhere, two Doberman Pinschers appeared and began doing their best to devour me. I lurched back to avoid their snapping jaws and fell off the wall. Luckily for me, I landed on Paula. Not so lucky for Paula. When we hit the ground, Paula let out a shriek and you could hear all the air rush out of her body. This poor girl had just taken the brunt of my weight on top of her. She was writhing on the ground in pain and gasping for air. I was terrified. I looked at Irwin and he was standing close by and laughing uncontrollably. It was right at this moment I realized that my good friend, Irwin Berniker, was bent and was not a good influence on me. Shortly after this I spent less and less time with him, partly because I was smarter and partly because I was working more and more.

I did contact him about two years ago. We had a great long chat on the phone. We made plans to see each other the next time I was in town. He inherited his mom and dad's home and lived there with his wife and children.

This is where Bert Michaels comes into the picture. I had just got a job singing and dancing in a new stage musical starring Milo O'Shea, an Irish star who had just come to America. It was being mounted in San Bernardino, which is about seventy-five miles outside of Los Angeles. Transportation was going to be a problem for me. This was when my crazy friend, Irwin Berniker, left me a parting gift of sorts. Irwin offered me his old Fiat for $300 and I jumped at it. I was extremely excited. My first car in Los Angeles, bought with my own money. Now I did not have to rely on anyone to get myself around.

On the very first drive to rehearsal in San Bernardino, this parting gift from Irwin Berniker, the mighty Fiat, suddenly started to cough and sputter halfway to San Bernardino and died. I rolled to a stop off the highway, and it suddenly burst into flames and burned to a crisp. The police and a fire truck came right away and extinguished the blaze. I was not only disgusted, but I was also worried about getting to rehearsal. Fortunately for me, a cast member, Bert Michaels, was driving by on his way to the same rehearsal. He very kindly offered to drive me there. By that time the police had called a tow truck and were loading up the Fiat carcass. After much begging, the police said that I could go. They said they would be in touch, and I would have to pay the tow truck costs. I thanked them and headed off to rehearsal with Bert Michaels. After rehearsal, Bert offered to drive me home. Thus began my friendship with Bert. The strange thing about the Fiat episode was that the police and the tow truck company never contacted me at all. It was like it had never happened. I have no explanation for this magical moment in my life.

Bert Michaels was in the movie *West Side Story* (1961) as Snowboy, one of the Jets. He starred in *Saturday Night Fever* (1977) as Pete, and in *Enchanted* (2007), with Amy Adams, as Dancer. He was a spectacular dancer. His stories about *West Side Story* (1961) intrigued me immensely. Little did I know that my future would include being cast as Arab in *West Side Story* (1961) in Vancouver, BC. He was a great guy and incredibly talented. He had a good voice, and he was a terrific actor. His companion was a beautiful Doberman Pinscher, named Elly, who went everywhere with him. My introduction to her was after the first rehearsal of the show. We were getting into his car and as I reached in, Elly wrapped her jaws around my wrist and would not let go until Bert told her to do so. This was scary because she could have easily snapped my arm in two. From that moment on, Elly was loving and gentle. Elly was one of the smartest dogs I have every met. At Bert's Hollywood apartment, I was praising Elly to Bert. He said, "Watch this!" We were in the living room, and he told Elly to go into the kitchen and wait for him. Elly promptly left the room. We waited for at least five minutes before going into the kitchen. There was Elly, sitting and waiting. He told her to go into the bathroom and wait for him. Off she went. We waited another five minutes and walked into the bathroom. Elly was there waiting. Amazing!

Bert generously gave me a ride to and from rehearsal and the show and brought me home every night. He was a truly kind, generous guy. Shortly after closing the show, he was cast in a remount of *Gypsy* (1962), on Broadway, and I lost contact with him. I hope he is doing well.

Walter Painter

Walter Painter- Dancer/ Choreographer/ Director/ Producer/ Writer

Walter is highly successful dancer, choreographer, director, writer, and producer. He has won three prime time Emmys for his choreographic work. His body of work is extensive. Walter always worked hard for everything he accomplished. He has earned every bit of his success. I love Walter and his wife Charlene. Walter and I were always together in our early days of struggling to get ahead.

We were best friends. I love Walter. Charlene, Walter, and I were always together, struggling to get ahead. We often got together to have dinner, sing songs, and dance whenever we could. Walter and I did so many gigs together. We worked a lot with Toni Basil. In fact, Toni, Walter, and I danced as a trio on many shows, including the *Dick Cavett Show* (1968), the *Merv Griffin Show* (1962), and others I have forgotten. In 1964, Walter and I were hired to perform in *West Side Story* (1961) at the Queen Elizabeth Theatre in Vancouver, BC. Walt played Action and I played Arab. That was the production where I met my soon to be wife, Charlene. Walter and I worked with David Winters a lot. We did *West Side Story* (1961) at the Valley Music Theatre and at the Hawaii Civic Light Opera House. Walter also played Action in the Theatre in the Round tour in Anaheim, San Diego, and San Carlos with my wife, Charlene, and star Pat Boone.

Recently, at the yearly Professional Dancers Society Awards luncheon, I was able to watch Walter Painter receive an award for his body of work in dance. Such a great honour. I was so happy for him. To top it off, Ann-Margret presented his award to him.

Walter and I both have a long association with Ann-Margret. We both featured in her first Las Vegas Act and in her CBS television special, *From Hollywood With Love* (1969). We danced in her movie *The Swinger* (1966) and Walter went on to direct and choreograph her second act in Las Vegas, to enormous success.

Recently, during one of the Professional Dancers Society functions at the Beverly Hilton Hotel, Walter and his wife, who is also named Charlene, invited my wife, Charlene, and me to their house in the valley for dinner. What excitement. Walter, Charlene, and I had countless dinners together during our early years and this was an opportunity to have another one after so many years apart. It was like no time had passed at all. We had a lovely dinner. We reminisced and sang songs like we used to do, just as if we were on a corner in South Philadelphia. That was the way it was in our younger days in Hollywood. I got to see Walter and Charlene again last Spring when Toni Basil received her award for her body of choreographic work and her innovative contributions to the business. David Winters was there to honour Toni and to promote his book *Tough Guys Do Dance* (2018). It was a great reunion. All of us were together again, in the lobby lounge, reminiscing with Walter, Toni Basil, Anita Mann,

Lesley Evans, Jill Gordon, Pete Menefee, Pam Freeman, Adele Yoshioka, Kate Kahn, and Sandhal Bergman. Once again, it was like no time had passed since 1971. Walter and I were very close in the 60s and early 70s. This is where it becomes bittersweet for me. I do not remember what happened at all, but Walter's and my friendship soured in the late 60s and it broke my heart. To this day, I do not know why or what happened. I have not asked him. I am not sure he remembers. I am going to talk to him about it the next time we meet, as I would love to get our friendship growing again.

Aretha Franklin

Aretha Franklin- Singer

My only encounter with the Queen of Soul, who is now in the arms of God, was in 1967 in Las Vegas. I was performing in the first Ann-Margret act at the Riviera Hotel. I was early one night for the late show, and I sat in one of the lounges just listening to the headliner band. The lead singer suddenly said that they had an incredibly special young recording artist in the audience. It was Aretha Franklin. She had just recorded her hit song, *Respect* (1967). She got up on stage and sang two songs for us. She was as sensational then as she was her entire career. Of course, we did not realise then that she would go on to have six decades of a stunning career. It truly was a special night.

Anita Mann

Anita Mann- Dancer/ Choreographer/ Director/ Producer

Anita Mann and I have been friends as far back as I can remember. She was a beautiful woman, a great dancer, and well respected as one of the most prolific choreographers in the business. Her list of her choreographic accomplishments is endless. She has five Prime Time Emmys to her credit. Our first time working together was in *West Side Story* (1961) in Vancouver, BC. She played Anybodys. We both travelled to Hawaii, where she reprised the same role. She also worked for David Winters many times on television series such as *Shindig* (1964) and *Hullaballoo* (1965). She danced in the *Beach Party* (1963) movies, and we both danced in the movie *Thoroughly Modern Millie* (1967). She was a pioneering choreographer in Las Vegas. Her show *Fantasy* (1999), at the Luxor, is still going strong after twenty-two years. Despite all of her success, she is one of the humblest people I know. She has become an icon in the business. She is a philanthropist, teacher, humanitarian, and mother. She is kind, generous, and, luckily for me, one of my best friends. She is still remarkably busy with her company, Anita Mann Productions. She recently founded a Dance Hall of Fame with director Louis J. Horvitz. Dancers and choreographers worldwide are finally in good hands and, because of Anita's and Louis's efforts, will get the recognition they duly deserve. She is a major force in the business.

Toni Basil

Toni Basil- Dancer/ Choreographer/ Director/ Film maker

Flat out, I love Toni Basil with all my heart. Toni is one of the most brilliant, talented artists I have ever met. She is beautiful, refreshingly honest, a maverick, and a visionary. I am forever grateful to her. She was a highly trained ballet, jazz, and tap dancer. She hired me as dancer, assistant choreographer, and she gave me my start as a choreographer. We have been friends since 1963. A substantial amount of my resume is jobs with Toni. We worked well together. Toni's mind was always racing at breakneck speed, and I had the ability to remember everything she produced. I remember many nights at Toni's house, with her sitting in second position on the floor with little pieces of wadded up paper representing the dancers. She would move them around as she choreographed. Toni had the ability to choreograph like this and the numbers always worked well. Through the years I have tried to set numbers this way, but it does not work for me. I have to go into the rehearsal space, turn on the music, and let it lead me.

Toni was always ahead of the curve. She usually led the way. She has worked with Tina Turner, the Beatles, David Bowie, and Bette

Midler, to name a few. One of her creations for the *Divine Ms. M* is a number with Bette and the dancers all dressed in mermaid costumes in wheelchairs. Simply stunning, and very funny!

We were doing all the dance styles of the times in the 60s, but Toni was always looking for something new. After I moved to Vancouver, some years later, I was working as entertainment director at a nightclub called Confetti. The club theme was New Years Eve every night. One day, Toni and I were talking on the telephone about my new job. I was always looking for new talent, dancers, jugglers, acrobats, unicyclists, buskers, or magicians to work at the club. She said that she had discovered a group of dancers out of Los Angeles and their specialty dance was Locking. The group's name was The Campbell lockers. Yes, the real Campbell Lockers! She said that they would be interested in coming to work for me at the club. It sounded perfect to me, and I brought them in as a headliner for two weeks. It was one of the best decisions I have ever made, but it was Toni who knew what they were. They tore the place up and the club was jammed with people for the entire two weeks. They were sensational! Fresh, new, and ahead of the curve. She has since been involved heavily in street dancing. She was one of the best Lockers out there. She travels the world, adjudicating street dance competitions. She is solely responsible for bringing street dancing mainstream. We all know how big street dancing is. Well, Toni was the queen of street dancing and respected as such. I am not surprised. This is Toni as I have always known her to be.

Recently, I had the extreme pleasure of attending the Professional Dancers Society yearly luncheon event at the Beverly Hills Hotel. Each year, the society honours dancers for their body of work in the business. This time they honoured Toni Basil, along with George Chakiris. David Winters flew in from Bangkok to be there for Toni. She was his assistant choreographer for a long time. Several members of the *West Side Story* (1961) movie and play cast were there, along with many of Toni's friends, including Walter Painter,

Pete Menefee, Lesley Evans, Anita Mann, Jill Gordon, Bobby Banas, Adele Yoshioka, Kate Kahn, Sandhal Bergman, and Sonja Haney.

After the show we all went into the lounge and reminisced for two hours. It was at least thirty to forty years since the last time we were all together in Hollywood. We talked and talked as we would have done forty years ago. As an added bonus, we noticed a legendary film star sitting at another table. It is true that you never know who you might see at the Beverly Hills Lounge. This time it was the one and only, Margaret O'Brien. Margaret won an Academy Award as a child actress in the film *Meet Me In St. Louis* (1944). She is still working today. We were not going to miss this opportunity. Several of us marched over to her table and introduced ourselves. She was very gracious, and she was pleased that we recognized her. It was a great Day.

Dick Foster

Dick Foster- Dancer/ Producer

I met Dick while working on the film *Gypsy* (1962). We became friends right away. Dick was a good tap dancer. We were in the Farmboy and the Eton numbers. After filming ended, Dick and I were together all the time. Dick had boundless energy and no end of ideas. He was born to be a producer. One of our enterprises, which was his idea, of course, was to sell records to music stores to promote recording artists trying to get known. He was always the entrepreneur. We parted ways for a while and did not see each other for a couple of years, not until after Charlene and I were married. He married Nicky, the legendary singer, Peggy Lee's daughter. During our time apart, he was always working towards being a producer. One day he called me, out of the blue, and asked me to come to his office at Bob Banner Productions. Bob Banner Productions produced the *Carol Burnett Show* (1967) and *Here's Peggy Fleming* (1968), which highlighted the Olympic gold medal ice skating star. Dick had worked his way up in the company and he had become the producer of *Peggy Fleming at Sun Valley* (1971). He wanted to hear my ideas before offering me the job of choreographing the special. One number would be easy. Two male dancers, one of which was me, would be dancing with Peggy on an outdoor Olympic sized skating rink in Sun Valley Lodge. It would be filmed in front of a live audience. The only problem I could see was how the dancers would get any traction on the ice. He said that he and choreographer, Roland Dupree, had come up with the idea to use Hush Puppy golf shoes. He planned to take out all the spikes except for one in the toe and one in the heel. He would file them to a fine point, and this would provide traction, and the dancers could also turn on the ice. It was brilliant. We used this idea, and it turned out great. The start of that number was exciting. Peggy was at one end of the ice, and we entered from the other end, running towards Peggy. We hit the ice in a dancer's split, rolled over to our stomachs, slid about forty feet, and we popped up right next to Peggy. The number was an immense success! The special won two prime time Emmys and my number was highly critically acclaimed.

The second number was more of a problem. Peggy's main guest star was Jean Claude Killy, the multiple Olympic gold medal winning skier. Dick wanted me to create a production number featuring both of their skills. I told him I would have to think about it and get back to him with my ideas. Normally, for me, all I needed was the theme of the number. I would turn on the music and let the music lead me. This was the only time I ever dreamed of the number overnight. The next day I called Dick and told him I had the number. We met two days later, and he loved the idea. My idea was that everything Peggy and the two male skaters did on the ice would be countered by Jean Claude and two female skiers on snow. It was a challenge number. At the end, Jean Claude would ski onto the ice surface and join Peggy for the finale.

Jean Claude and the two girls wore short skis. Dick loved the idea. I was set. Dick hired me and I had to learn to ski in a hurry. Now, in Los Angeles, there was not much snow. However, there were fake slopes where you could learn the basics. The synthetic slope was filled with small plastic chips that simulated snow. I had only two lessons before heading to Sun Valley. There, I had only one day on the bunny slope to get comfortable on real snow. Talk about a rush. I was struggling by myself on the slope, and a skier stopped and asked me what I was doing. I told him I had to learn to ski quickly. He stayed with me for about an hour and a half. He showed me the rhythm of traversing and, suddenly, I had it. Traversing was just like changing direction right to left on the dance floor. I was just a beginner, but I could ski! This man, whom I did not know at all, was one of the angels in my life. Without him, who knows what might have happened. What a gift he gave me.

Jean Claude was coming the next day and I would be to telling him and the girls what to do. I should have been terrified, but I have to say I was not. I have always just done it, just jumped in and swam away. Jean Claude and the two girls, who were training to compete in the next Olympics could do everything I asked of them and more. We created so many unusual moves. They were fabulous. Peggy's choreographer for all her specials was Bob Paul. Bob was also a great skater on the world stage and helped with the skating portion of the number. The result was such a success. The editing of my number was brilliant. The special won two prime time Emmys.

One for the director, Sterling Johnson, and one for the director of photography, Robert E. Collins.

Dick Foster and I were inseparable again. Dick Foster and his wife, Nicky, would invite us to their home in Beverly Hills. Their home was next to Dick's mother-in-law's house, on her property. Did I mention her name was Peggy Lee, the famous recording star? We got to meet her. She was so gracious and lovely. Dick travelled with Peggy's live show for many years as her road manager. We would go to Dick and Nicky's home, swim all day, have dinner, and then play poker into the wee hours of the morning. Our daughter would have sleepovers with their kids. Sometimes we would all stay over, usually when Peggy was on the road. Charlene and I slept in Peggy Lee's bed many times. Wow! Crazy fun times.

Dick went on to become one of the most successful producers in Las Vegas for many years. I lost touch with him. I heard he sold all his vast holdings in Las Vegas and moved somewhere near Seattle. I want to see him again and will track him down. I need to reconnect.

David Winters

David winters- Dancer/ Actor/ Choreographer/
Director/ Producer/ Film maker

There is so much to tell about David Winters. He began as an actor/dancer in England. After coming to America, he landed the role of Baby John in the first Broadway production of *West Side Story* (1961). He went on to play Arab in the movie version. From there, he went on to become one of the most successful dancers, choreographer, director, producer, writers in the business. He has worked with everybody. Fortunately for me, he did most of his work when I was in Los Angeles. I took classes from him at the Coronet Theatre on La Cienega Boulevard in West Hollywood. David first hired me to dance in the film *The Swinger* (1966), starring Ann-Margret and Anthony Franciosa. I fell in love with his style because it fit me so well. It was fresh, current, and full of life. Next, he hired me to dance in an Elvis Presley film *Easy Come Easy Go* (1967). In this film, he had to leave before principal filming was finished. He asked me to stage the "Setting of the Picnic Table" sequence with Elvis and the cast. By doing this, he furthered my career in choreography. He hired me to perform in Nancy Sinatra's television special *Movin' with Nancy* (1967). In this show, Pete Menefee and I got to do a featured dance section with David. This was incredibly special. It was extremely hard and exciting work. This special was directed by Jack Haley Junior, who was Jack Haley's son. You may remember Jack Haley Senior playing the Tin Man in *The Wizard of Oz* (1939). Next, David hired me to perform in Ann-Margret's first Las Vegas act. Our opening number with Ann was on Triumph motorcycles. We took Las Vegas by storm. Shortly after that, David asked me to reprise my role in the CBS superspecial of Ann's act that we had done in Las Vegas. Every job I have done with David has been ground-breaking, important work. He was truly a visionary genius. I loved him and before he passed on, he told me that I was one of his favorite dancers and that he thought I was great. I consider this very generous of one of our giants in the business. Last year, in the spring, David travelled to Los Angeles to honour Toni Basil. She was receiving a lifetime achievement award for her outstanding contributions as a dancer, choreographer, director, producer, and visionary. Toni was David's assistant choreographer. He gave Toni her start, just like she gave me mine. She truly gave me the break I needed by encouraging Dick Clark Productions to hire me as choreographer for their ABC Studios hit television series *Where The Action Is* (1965).

Prior to the event for Toni, David and I had not seen or talked to each other for forty-six years. Talk about an electrically charged reunion. We talked, laughed, cried, and schmoozed for three hours. That same afternoon, David, Walter Painter, Toni, Lesley Evans, and I got to meet the famous film star, Margaret O'Brien. It was a magical time. Since then, we have been in constant contact on Facebook. Our angels were working for us, even working overtime.

Pam Freeman (Parker)

Pam Freeman/Parker- Dancer/ Actor

Pam Freeman was a successful actress and one of the best dancers I have worked with. She was the quintessential girl next door. She was a blonde, blue-eyed beauty. Once you met her, you just wanted to be with her. In 1962, after we both graduated from High School, we took dance classes together at a studio on Fairfax Drive in Hollywood. Our instructor was Alex Plasschaert. I have mentioned him before. He was one of the major mentor/teachers in my life. Alex had guest teachers occasionally, including Nick Navarro and the famous dancer and film star, Juliette Prowse.

The 60s was filled with work. Pam recently reminded me of some work we did together, including the film *Beach Party* (1963), with Frankie Avalon and Annette Funicello, *Pajama Party* (1964), with Tommy Kirk and Annette Funicello, and Elvis's movies *Clambake* (1967) and *Speedway* (1968). She was also a featured dancer on the television series *Shindig* (1964) and played Phyllis Diller's daughter on *The Pruitts of South Hampton* (1966). We also danced together in the Ann-Margret film *The Swinger* (1966).

Pam once said that dancers have a bond that cannot be broken. She was so right. Pam is one of the nicest women I know. At the first Professional Dancers Society Gypsy Awards, she was the one who met me at the door, stayed with me, introduced me to folks, and made sure I was comfortable She is one classy lady! We were the best of friends dancing together in the 60s, and we are even closer friends today. I cherish our friendship!

Teri Garr

Teri Garr- Dancer/ Actor/ Film star

Teri began as a trained dancer in both ballet and jazz. We worked together in Elvis Presley films, Nancy Sinatra's television special, the stage production of *West Side Story* (1961), and we both had an acting part together on an episode of the television series *Batman* (1966). She also a danced on the *Tami Show* (1964), *Shindig* (1964), *Hullabaloo* (1966), *Shivaree* (1965), and in the *Beach Party* (1963) movies. After all those early dancing jobs, Teri became a major movie star. Her quirky, lightning wit attracted movie producers who presented her in films such as *Close Encounters of the Third Kind* (1977), *Young Frankenstein* (1974), Francis Ford Coppola's *One From The Heart* (1981), and *Tootsie* (1982), where she was nominated for an Academy Award for Best Supporting Actor.

Teri was a beautiful woman, inside and out. We have remained the best of friends throughout. I have been able to see her each time I have visited to Los Angeles for the Professional Dancer Society Gypsy Awards. Unfortunately, in 1990, she was diagnosed with Multiple Sclerosis and has not been able to perform much since. She has still retained her lightning quick wit and wonderful sense of humour. Unfortunately, recently, Teri Garr lost her battle with MS. I will never laugh the same way again. I love her dearly.

Suzanne Charney

Suzanne Charney- Dancer

Suzanne was one of the best dancers I never worked with. I met her when I auditioned for the movie *Sweet Charity* (1969). She was the star dancer in the "Rich Man's Frug" number. I did get to dance next to her at the audition, but I had to leave after getting sick in front of Bob Fosse. I really should never have auditioned at all because I could have given the flu to others there. I just could not bear the thought of missing the opportunity to dance for Bob Fosse. We still became friends through it all. She was one of the nicest people I have ever met. I regret not collaborating with her. Next time I am in Los Angeles, we will get together and reminisce.

Dom Deluise

Dom Deluise- Comic/ Actor

Two years after I finished filming *Hello Dolly* (1969), I was hired to dance on an episode of the *Dean Martin Show* (1965) at NBC. Dom was a regular guest on the show. I was a great fan of his zany style of comedy and was excited to meet him. He was so friendly that we became fast friends. He and his wife were brand new parents, and my wife and I just had our second child. Both moms were breast feeding and Dom was excited to know what mother's milk tasted like. He asked me if I knew what it tasted like. I said I did not know. He said he was afraid to try. He then asked me to try it and to let him know the next day what it was like. The next day I told him that I had imbibed! He laughed like crazy. The next day, at rehearsals, he ran up to me and told me that he had imbibed, and it was fabulous. He then told Dean Martin the story and Dean roared with laughter. Dom was a charming, funny, and kind man. I thoroughly enjoyed meeting him.

Donald O'Connor

Donald O'Connor- Dancer/ Actor/ Film star

Donald O'Connor was one of the greatest singer/dancer/actors of all time. In 1967, I was hired to dance in his nightclub act. We performed at Harrah's, in Reno, for two weeks from January 5 to January 22. It was a spectacular time for me. He was very respectful of me. He said he loved my dancing. He said I reminded him of himself when he was younger. He even featured me in a tap number with him. The number included a tap challenge between him and me. I was doing trades, whereby Donald would improvise one or two counts of eight and I would respond with one or two counts of eight of my own. It was structured within a fully choreographed tap number with all six dancers in the show. The tap challenge could be long or short in length, depending on what Donald wanted to do. The number always brought down the house. His entire act was sensational!

An amazing thing about Donald was that, after the late show, he would invite all of us, including the crew, to have some food and drinks in his suite every night. He would sing and dance, play the piano, and tell jokes until he was exhausted. I was in show business heaven, but I have to say it was a bit odd. At the end of the run, he gave us all parting gifts. He gave me a set of his taps that he had used while filming *Singin' in the Rain* (1952). What a treasure for me. He was kind and very generous. This was another moment in my life that proved, beyond a shadow of a doubt, that if you work hard and keep your dreams in clear sight, they can come true.

Robert Wagner and Raquel Welch

Robert Wagner and Raquel Welch- Actors/ Film Stars

Absolutely amazing things can happen when you least expect them to. I was incredibly pleased that Paul Becker had asked me to dance on an episode of the television series *Date My Dad* (2107) for WTN. By itself, this was not an unusual occurrence, but what was unusual was that I was going to be a dance double for none other than Robert Wagner. In my wildest of dreams, I have never seen myself as resembling anything like Robert Wagner. Paul obviously saw something different. At rehearsals, we began to learn the ballroom dance that Mr. Wagner and Raquel Welch would do. Not only was I excited to meet Mr. Wagner, but also over the moon with the advent of meeting Raquel Welch. Raquel arrived at rehearsals before Robert. She was drop dead gorgeous. At first, she was a bit nervous, probably because she did not know what the choreographer was going to ask her to do. Soon, after seeing what we had set, she relaxed and was as professional as anyone I have worked with. She had a profound sense of humour, both of her feet firmly on the ground, and was respectful towards the choreographer and dancers. When Mr. Wagner arrived. he was as handsome as ever. He was quite relaxed and friendly. The rehearsal with them did not last long, as they had other things to do.

On the day of shooting, I sat down in the makeup chair and the makeup artists began to do their magic. It took three full hours. They had to cut and fit the wig I was to wear to look exactly like Mr. Wagner's hair. When they finished, I did not recognize myself in the mirror. Here was a man with great hair who looked handsome. I was overwhelmed. I was dressed in the exact suit Robert was wearing. As I was walking to the set, Robert Wagner was coming toward me. He looked at me in the hallway and suddenly stopped. He said to me, "You look good. You look just like me." This happened twice. After the second time, we both broke into great laughter. He liked looking at himself, so to speak. He was very charming. The rest of the day was great fun. I enjoyed everyone on the show. My dance partner looked stunning. She was beautiful in her own right, but also looked great as Raquel's double. As I mentioned earlier, amazing things can happen!

Kenny Ortega

Kenny Ortega- Dancer/ Choreographer/ Director/ Producer/ Writer

Kenny was a giant in the business. He has had worldwide success as a dancer, choreographer, director, writer, and producer. You can see his work in films such as *Xanadu* (1980), *Pretty in Pink* (1986), *Ferris Bueller's Day Off* (1986), *Dirty Dancing* (1987), the *High School Musical* (2006) trilogy, the *Descendants* (2015) trilogy, Michael Jackson's *This is It* (2009), and the television series *Julie and the Phantoms* (2020). His accomplishments speak for themselves, along with his talent and drive to succeed. Kenny was much more than that. He was one of the kindest humans I have ever met. He loved artists. He was a born mentor. He remembered where he came from. He remembered how hard it was to succeed in this business. His work ethic was unquestioned.

At the first audition for *Descendants* (2015), Kenny watched me dance and then told everybody in the room, "We have to find a part for this guy." Now, I have heard a lot of this kind of rhetoric throughout my career and most of it has never panned out. With some people, talk is cheap. With Kenny, it was not just talk. He was true to his word, which is rare indeed! He found a part for me. Extraordinary! Since then, he has featured me in both *Descendants* (2015) and *Descendants 3* (2019), as well as in the Netflix television series *Julie and the Phantoms* (2020).

Before meeting Kenny during casting sessions for *Descendants* (2015), we had never worked together. We had worked with a lot of the same people, but our paths had just never crossed. When we met, it seemed like he was someone I had known my entire life. We became friends right away. At the wrap party for *Descendants* (2015), we did some impromptu tap dancing for the cast and crew. Now, each time we are together, we end up doing a few tap combos just for the sheer joy of it. If you are ever fortunate enough to meet Kenny Ortega, you will love him as much as I do.

Ken Gibson

Ken Gibson - Producer CBC

Ken Gibson was the senior producer at CBC Studios, in Vancouver, BC. Between the years 1976 through 1984, most of my work at the CBC was a result of meeting Ken Gibson. My history at the CBC started with a co-production of the *Wolfman Jack* (1976) television series. I danced on this series and co-choreographed it. This led to me choreographing the *Rene Simard Show* (1977), which was co-produced by Alan Thicke. Alan Thicke took me to Toronto to choreograph Anne Murray's *Ladies Night* (1978) television show. Ken Gibson also introduced me to Patsy Macdonald, CBC producer, who signed me to choreograph the *Canadian Express* (1977) television series, which showcased Canadian recording artists. I was able to feature my dancers in different locales across Canada with this series. Ken later hired me to choreograph *The Raes* (1978) and a CBC Christmas special featuring Juliette. Both shows were directed by Michael Watt. I also choreographed a television special starring Carroll Baker, a Canadian country music star, and another television special guest starring legendary Canadian actor, Bruno Gerussi. My work on these projects led me to dance on the *Mr. Candyman* (1978) special, starring the legendary singer and civil rights activist, Leon Bibb. Some days I would be choreographing three projects at the same time. I would rehearse one show from 9:00am to 1:00pm, then another from 2:00pm to 5:00pm, and the third from 6:00pm to 9:00pm. It was crazy busy.

As you can see, the body of my work at the CBC was a result of Ken Gibson's support and guidance. It shows us repeatedly that we can not do it alone. Ken Gibson was one of my angels who furthered my career. He was a consummate gentleman, honest to the core, and his extensive career at the CBC proved his rare ability to know what the audiences wanted, and he knew how to give it to them.

Ken retired from the CBC in 1997. Recently, we had a lovely reunion at his beautiful home, on the waters edge, in an upscale area of Vancouver called Point Grey. Many of the producers, directors, directors of photography, dancers, makeup artists, and stars we worked with from those days at the CBC attended. It was a spectacular day!

Savion Glover

Savion Glover- Dancer/ Actor/ Choreographer

In 1995, Charlene and I took an actual vacation to Toronto for our niece's wedding. From there, we travelled on to New York City. What a wonderful experience it was. Through one of my work colleagues, we secured a charming bed and breakfast apartment about five blocks from Times Square. I had not been to New York since working on the *Leslie Uggams Show* (1969) many years prior. We saw two Broadway shows, *Forever Tango* (1995), and a production of Savion Glover's show *Bring in 'da Noise, Bring in 'da Funk* (1995). After seeing Savion's show I arranged to have a tap class with one of the show's stars, Omar Edwards, at the Broadway Dance Centre. On the day of the class, approximately twenty-five other tappers and I were all in the studio waiting for Omar to arrive. Omar was late. The girl from the front desk said that Omar did not feel like teaching today. I asked if there was going to sub. She said there would not be a sub, but we could use the hour to jam with each other. I decided to leave. I was not coming all this way to New York to not have a class. Besides, I could have just gone down the street to another studio and taken a class from someone else. As I was taking off my shoes, I noticed someone walk past me with one sock on and one sock off. I stood up and saw that it was Savion Glover. He said that he would sub for Omar. What a treat! The best tap dancer in the world was going to conduct the class. It was a blast and a half. As we were learning the combination, Savion came over and spent some one-on-one time with me to get the right sounds for one of the steps. I was honoured! He broke down one part of the combo to its bare knuckles. I still dance this combination to this day. I spoke to Savion after the class and thanked him. He was so gracious and a class act. The following day, I took a class from one of the Australian Tap Dogs. We danced a combination to Kenny Loggins "Footloose." Once the fast, difficult routine was set, we started to dance it. Suddenly, he asked me where I was from. I told him I was from Vancouver, and he admonished his class, saying they were having trouble with this combination, but a guy comes in from nowhere and has no trouble doing the dance at all. A nice compliment. In the last fifteen minutes of class, he asked if I would dance it with him while his class watched. Not only did we turn it on, but we were challenging each other throughout the dance. Both of us were sweating profusely, exhausted, and gasping for air by the end of one of the best classes I had had in years. It was a thrill.

There were so many more wonderful artists I have known and worked with, including Buddy Ebsen on *The Beverly Hillbillies* (1962), Carol Channing in *Thoroughly Modern Millie* (1967), Dom Deluise on *The Dean Martin Show* (1971), Bobby Rydell in *Bye Bye Birdie* (1963), Yvonne Craig in *Kissin' Cousins* (1964), Deborah Kerr in *Marriage on the Rocks* (1965), Vivian Vance on *Here's Lucy* (1967), James Brown on *Where the Action Is* (1964), David Arquette in *A Very Merry Muppet Christmas Movie* (2002), and Raquel Welch in *Date My Dad* (2017). I have also had the good fortune to meet and work with Julie Andrews, Mary Tyler Moore, James Fox, Bea Lillie, Jack Soo, Dean Martin, Dick Van Dyke, Janet Lee, Paul Lynde, Elvis

Presley, Caesar Romero, Bob Hope, Frankie Avalon, Diana Ross and the Supremes, Bobby Freeman, Joan Cusack, Robert Wagner, Rich Little, Donald O'Connor, Gene Nelson, Ray Bolger, Ann Murray, Mel Torme, Paul Anka, Rene Simard, Michael Crawford, Tommy Tune, Francis Ford Coppola, Louie Prima, Christopher Lloyd, Phil Harris, Alice Faye, Steve Allen, Leslie Nielson, Dionne Warwick, Tina Turner, Neil Patrick Harris, Dick Clark, Nancy Sinatra, Mickey Rooney, Petula Clark, Jack Cassidy, Johnny Carson, Merv Griffin, Toni Basil, and John Cena. Every one of these people amazed and inspired me to do and be better.

I have always been star struck. In every case, I was where I wanted to be. The stars accepted me and helped put me at ease. I found that every one of them were friendly, helpful, kind and, of course, immensely talented.

Chapter Nine

Ann-Margret

Ann-Margret and James Hibbard, 1967

I first met Ann-Margret while dancing in the film *Bye Bye Birdie* (1963). Talk about drop dead beautiful! Ann was, and still is, gorgeous. Just being in Ann-Margret's presence, you could feel her passion. She was a superstar ready to explode. Nothing could stop her. She was always going full tilt. Ann-Margret was completely professional. Her work ethic was infectious and if you did not up your game you would be left in the dust. She was very respectful of dancers. You could not help but fall in love with her. My luck was that we became friends while working on the film. We all know how her performance just jumped off the screen and launched her into super stardom. We were extremely fortunate to meet and work with her. Every working, young dancer in Hollywood was in *Bye Bye Birdie* (1963). From start to finish, it was great fun. I am happy that it was just the first of many experiences of working with Ann-Margret.

Ann-Margret and Bobby Rydell in *Bye Bye Birdie*, 1963

The next time I worked with Ann-Margret was when chore-ographer David Winters hired me to dance in the movie *Viva Las Vegas* (1964). Although this was my second film with Ann-Margret, it was my first with the King, Elvis Presley. David hired me again to dance in her film *The Swinger* (1966), with Anthony Franciosa. David Winters choreography was so vibrant and new. What a wonderful talent he was.

Ann-Margret and James Hibbard in *The Swinger*, 1966

My good fortune just kept coming with the next project, Ann-Margret's first Las Vegas act at the Riviera Hotel in 1967. David, once again, took on the role of directing and choreographing. If you thought her film performances were explosive, on stage she was a napalm bomb. She was compelling. We had a tremendous time while we were in Las Vegas. What a great job this was. Every male dancer in Los Angeles wanted to be in this show. It was considered a coup and a great professional compliment to get this job. The opening number was on Triumph 650 motorcycles! Ann was an accomplished rider. Her act took Las Vegas by storm. It was so exciting to do. We all felt on top of the world. Every time you worked with Ann-Margret you were on top of the world.

Cast of Ann-Margret Act-Riviera Hotel, Las Vegas,1967

In all, there were eight dancers and four singers hired for a six-week run. Ann called us her "Gentlemen." The cast consisted of dancers Pete Menefee, Walter Painter, Gus Trikonis, Roger Minami, Joe Cassini, and Birl Johns, and me, and singers, John Harris, Larry Billman, Warren Hays, and Fred Barton. Ann-Margret's assistant was the sensational ex-dancer, Maggie Banks. Maggie was a highly successful dancer with a resume which included the movie *West Side Story* (1961), *The Andy Williams Show* (1962), and *The Dinah*

Shore Chevy Show (1956). She was wonderful to work with. One night, during rehearsals, we went to shoot publicity photos in the basement of an old building. This was a new experience for me. It was a blast. All the motorcycles we rode in the act were there. There were all kinds of lighting setups installed. We shot hundreds of photos. The music of the evening was by The Moody Blues, such as "Nights In White Satin." It set a great mood. David Winters brought in lots of food, beer, and wine, and the party was on!

The day after we opened at the Riviera Hotel, we were the talk of the town. Everywhere we went we were treated like royalty. We were riding high. One night, David Merrick, one of the most acclaimed Tony Award winning Broadway producers, saw our act and afterwards came into our dressing room. He wanted to speak to Walter Painter and me. Good grief! Without delay, he offered both of us work in one of two shows he was producing on Broadway. I do not even remember the show names. We were so cocky. In the dressing room, we boldly asked him what the pay was. When he told us, we both said no thank you. We were making twice as much with Ann-Margret. We told him, "We'll stick with our Annie!" He understood and told us to let him know if we changed our minds. We did not change our minds.

Ann-Margret Act, Riviera Hotel, Las Vegas, 1967

Ann-Margret Act, Riviera Hotel, Las Vegas, 1967

Ann-Margret Act, Riviera Hotel, Las Vegas, 1967

The act generated such acclaim. David Winters sold the show to CBS Television Studios for a television special. It was titled *Ann-Margret: From Hollywood with Love (1969) and* would feature segments of the act and guest stars such as Lucille Ball and Dean Martin. David Winters directed and choreographed the special. To our great good fortune, David Winters brought us all back to do it. He also added a new dancer, Carl Coppock, to join us. It was one of the best jobs I have ever been part of. David garnered a Prime-Time Emmy nomination for outstanding achievement in choreography, which was new in television.

Unfortunately for me, this would be the last time I worked with Ann-Margret and David Winters. Within a year after we finished taping the special, my family and I moved to Canada.

From Hollywood With Love poster, 1968

Ann-Margret, James Hibbard, and dancers in
From Hollywood With Love, 1968

Ann-Margret and James Hibbard in *From Hollywood With Love,* 1968

Recently, I had a wonderful reunion with Ann-Margret at the Professional Dancers Society Gypsy Awards event at the Beverly Hilton Hotel in Beverly Hills. Some of my best friends, including Walter Painter, Miriam Nelson, and Alan Johnson were getting awards for their body of work in choreography. To top it off, Ann-Margret was there to present their awards. Now, you must realize that I had not seen Ann for more than forty years.

As I was walking up to get my tickets, a publicity agent, Wayne Shulman, came up and asked me if I was Jimmy Hibbard (this was my working name in Hollywood). He said that he knew of my work, and he showed me a photo of Ann and me, which I had never seen. I asked him if I could have the photograph. He politely refused my request but said that he had brought Ann-Margret and her husband, Roger Smith, to the event that day. He asked if I would like to meet up with her later. I said, "Hell yes! I haven't seen her in at least forty years." After the show, Wayne told me that Ann-Margret was getting ready to leave and, if I wanted to see her, now was the best time. She was facing the stage when Wayne told her that there was somebody here whom she might remember from her past. She turned around and in less than a second she said, "Jimmy Hibbard, what the f*ck happened to you?" I explained that I had moved to Canada, and she said, "You were one of my gentlemen. You were the best dancer in Hollywood!"

What a thrilling moment! Ann was always kind and very generous. It had been at least forty years since I saw her last, and we had a wonderful talk. We reminisced for about twenty minutes. I got to speak with her husband, Roger Smith, who was extremely sick. I told her that I loved her since the day I met her. She told me that she loved me too. We both cried a bit. Annie was one of my angels. I am still in love with her!

Just like the lyrics, *I feel as though I am sitting here doing the Sunday Times crossword puzzle and somehow the words won't come* from "Starting Here Starting Now", writing my story is most often difficult for me to do.

Chapter Ten

Lucille Ball

The Lucy Show logo, 1962

I had the honour and pleasure of working on Lucy's television series *The Lucy Show* (1962). I have a few stories about being on the show. I danced and sang on six or seven shows. Jack Baker choreographed all episodes. I loved Lucy. She was in total control. Every morning the director, lighting designer, director of photography, costume designer, dancers, choreographer, singers, guest artists, and anyone else involved with each segment would meet. We sat at a long table with director chairs on both sides. At one end was a tall director chair where Lucy sat. Lucy would go through the entire script and hear ideas from each of the department heads. They discussed what they planned to do, and Lucy would respectfully say what she wanted. That was that. Talk about being in control.

She gave us all a gift at the end of each show. During one rehearsal, I was asked what time it was by another dancer. I did not have a wristwatch at the time. Lucy remembered this, and my gift from her was a Timex wristwatch. Other gifts I remember included a box of candy and a gold necklace chain. She was very thoughtful. She was as professional as anyone I have ever seen. I admired her so. You could not help but fall in love with her. At the last show I danced on for her, she called me over to her and told me how much she loved my work and my dedication. She kissed me on each cheek. This was another moment in my career where someone I loved, and respected, told me I was on the right track when I needed it most.

One day, shortly after filming of one of the shows, I was driving Charlene and our daughter, Gianna, to a shopping mall. We had stopped at a light, at the corner of Melrose Avenue and Caheunga Boulevard, where Desilu Studio was. While waiting for the light to change, I noticed a Rolls Royce pull up on my left. I looked over as the passenger window was being rolled down. A gloved hand began waving at us through the open window. To my astonishment, it was Lucille Ball! She said, "Hi, Jimmy," and asks how I was. She had her mother with her, and we had our daughter with us. I introduced Lucy and her mom to Charlene and Gianna. Lucy introduced her mother to us. Wow! The light changed to green, but Lucy just continued to talk, reminiscing about the show we just did. The people behind us started to honk, so I said to Lucy, "I think we should go." Lucy just laughed and said, "Don't worry. I own this street and we can talk as long as we want." This was amazing! Then she said, "You're right, we should probably go." We waved at each other as Lucy turned left into Desilu Studios, and we proceeded to go to the shopping mall. I will never forget that moment. Just imagine, Lucille Ball!

On one episode of *The Lucy Show* (1962), the legendary song and dance man, John Bubbles, was one of the guest stars. John Bubbles was known as the Father of Rhythm Tap and had great fame in the movies in the late 30s and 40s with his partner, Buck. They were billed as Buck and Bubbles. Buck would play the piano and Bubbles would dance. Both sang and, sometimes, Buck would dance with

Bubbles. John Bubbles was a great tap artist. He added more heel work than Bill Robinson usually did. One time, during rehearsals, Mr. Bubbles was warming up. I was avidly watching him from about four feet away. He would do a step and I would ask him to repeat it. He would say, "Nope, it's boxed." Then he would do another, and I would ask him to do it again, slower. He would say, "Nope, it's boxed." Then he held out his hand and said, "But you can pay me, and I'll show it to you again." I suddenly understood that he was encouraging me to steal it. These legendary tappers cultivated their styles over many years and were not about to give it away. To this day, if you have the chops, your job is to steal a step that looks good to you and make it your own. He was not nasty at all. He was just schooling me. I loved him from that moment on. I still use a couple of his steps in my performances to this day. I did steal them, and they always work.

Mel Torme, Lucille Ball and John Bubbles in
"Main Street USA" episode, *The Lucy Show,* 1966

On the same episode, "Main Street USA," I had the pleasure of working with the wonderful Mel Torme, also known as the Velvet Fog. He was a sensational jazz singer, scat artist, and writer of the famous Christmas song called "The Christmas Song." This was one of the most popular Christmas songs ever written. Everyone knows the lyrics *chestnuts roasting on an open fire, Jack Frost nipping at your nose.* For this one episode, he had written a song especially for the show. During rehearsals, he sat at the piano and sang it. All the dancers and the choreographer were sitting and listening to him. He said it was an easy song and, if anyone wanted to sing along, to please feel free to do so. He sang it a couple of times and then some of us started to sing along with him. I naturally harmonize and, when he heard me, he said he liked what I was doing, and he also liked what one of the girls was singing. To our astonishment he asked us to come to his home in San Fernando Valley and record it. Talk about being in seventh heaven when we went to his home. He had a fully equipped recording studio, where we recorded his tune for the show. Mel added more voices afterwards, and we also recorded on the set during shooting. We were even paid a guest artist's rate for being able to sing.

For me, there was something even greater at his home. Ever since I was a small boy, I wanted to be a cowboy. I wanted to ride horses and shoot six guns. Well, Mel Torme was a western gun collector. He had guns from the Civil War, Colt 45s, Smith and Wesson pistols, fast draw rigs, early repeating rifles, and even had a solid gold Colt 45. Unbelievable! I was in heaven. I did not want to leave. A couple of years later I did get a fast draw rigged holster and a Ruger six-gun. I practiced tirelessly for hours on end. I became quite good at it. That was as far as I took it. I never entered a fast draw competition. What a wonderful time with Mel Torme!

On another episode of the Lucy Show, titled "Viv Visits Lucy", I played a hippie dancer at a far out, right on, boss, tough, mighty rough club on the Sunset Strip. One of the stars, Vivian Vance, was a very funny, classy lady. She was gracious and friendly, but Lucy was the queen of television. Everyone knew it.

Vivian Vance and Lucille Ball, *The Lucy Show,* 1967

Recently, I watched a Nicole Kidman and Javier Bardham movie *Being the Ricardos* (2021). Initially, I was not sure I wanted to watch it, but it was superb. Ms. Kidman's and Mr. Bardham's portrayal of Lucy and Ricky was spot on. Nicole's characterization of Lucy was just as I remembered her. Smart, kind, supportive, and, to me, motherly. I was right back there, with my wife and daughter, sitting at the traffic light having a casual chat with the one and only Lucille Ball!

Chapter Eleven

Hawaii

After much success with productions of WSS in Vancouver-1964, California-1964, and Hawaii-1965, a great dancer friend of mine, Jim Hutchison, called and asked Charlene and me to join his production of *West Side Story* at the Hawaii Civic Light Opera. Walter Painter and Anita Mann were also invited. What a fantastic opportunity to travel to Hawaii once again, after being there in 1965. Jim was directing this production and his wife, Wisa D'Orso, was to play the role of Anita. Wisa was a beautiful, fiery brunette. She was a great dancer and singer. Jim signed me to choreograph and play Riff, the leader of the Jets. Anita Mann reprised the role of Anybodys, and Walter Painter reprised the role of Action. My wife, Charlene, reprised the role of Rosalia, and sang "Somewhere" for the ballet sequence. Charlene had just given birth to our first child, Gianna, and she was only six weeks old. During rehearsals, and the run of the show, we would need help in looking after Gianna. We decided to bring Charlene's Aunty Elma over to Hawaii to be Gianna's nanny. It sure proved to be the right decision.

During the rehearsal period, Gianna and Aunty Elma were at the theatre with us every day. My cue to take a break coincided with Charlene's feedings of Gianna. Charlene was breast feeding and when I saw her leaking through her top, I knew it was a suitable time to have a break. It was an extraordinary time. Our director, Jim Hutchison, was understanding and it all worked out well.

The run was highly successful and being in Hawaii was dreamlike. On one of our days off from the show, Charlene, Walter

Painter, Anita Mann, her husband, who came over to be with her during the show, and I went for an outing. One of the dancers, who lived in Hawaii, was our guide. We drove up onto the Pali, the Hawaiian word for cliff, in the mountains. There was a place there where the wind, which blows constantly, was so powerful it would hold you up if you leaned into it. I am sure that, if the wind suddenly stopped, we would have fallen to the ground. Our guide led us onto a trail in the mountains, which we followed single file, to a clearing where there were several pairs of jeans and water buckets lying around. It looked so odd. She told us to find a pair of jeans that fit, to put them on, and to get a bucket. We were perplexed. She instructed us to fill the bucket from the stream nearby and to come over to the edge of the hillside. We looked over the edge and we saw, what appeared to be, a mud trough which zigzagged down the mountain side. She told us to pour the bucket of water into this trough and to jump in. Holy smokes! It was like toad's wild ride down the mountain. It was an absolute thrill! We each did this several times, amid shrieks of sheer joy. By the end, we were tired and covered in mud. We took off the jeans and continued along this jungle trail. Suddenly, we came out to an enormous water fall which fell into a huge, deep, pool of water. It looked like something you might see in a travel brochure. It was in the middle of the jungle and so beautiful. We spent a couple of hours there, swimming and washing the mud from our bodies. What an amazing time we had. We returned home that night, had a lovely Hawaiian Luau at our hotel, went to bed, and slept like babies. After our successful run of West Side Story, Jim Hutchison and I went on to work together in several films including Thoroughly Modern Millie (1968) at Universal Film Studios and The One and Only Genuine Original Family Band (1968) at Disney Studios.

Charlene Brandolini and James Hibbard in Hawaii, 1966

During the run of the show, Wisa D'Orso, who played Anita, took sick for a few days and Charlene took over her role until she was feeling well enough to return. There was a lot of adjusting to do. Charlene was primarily a singer/actress who could move well. The role of Anita was a major dance role, so there was a lot of re-staging needed. We all met the task and Charlene carried it off well, being the major talent she was.

Jim Hutchison and I went on to work in many films together after *West Side Story* (1957) closed, including *Hello Dolly* (1964) and *The One And Only Genuine Original Family Band* (1968). Both Jim and his wife, Wisa, have since passed on. May they rest in peace. They were both lovely people.

Chapter Twelve

Frank and Nancy Sinatra

Marriage On The Rocks (1965)
Director - Jack Donohue
Writer - Cy Howard
Producer - William H. Daniels
Production Companies - A-C Productions, Sinatra Enterprises
Choreographer- Jonathan Lucas
Distributed by Warner Bros. Studios
Released - September 24, 1965

Marriage on the Rocks (1965) starred Frank Sinatra, Dean Martin, Deborah Kerr, and Nancy Sinatra. Most of the filming took place on the Warner Bros. studios lot in Burbank, California. Several dancers and I were hired to dance in the film. One time, we were on a break and the choreographer came and asked if any of us knew how to do the dances of the time. He was referring to dances such as the swim, the pony, the mashed potato, and the wobble. No one, besides me, raised their hand. The choreographer was Jonathan Lucas. He was not familiar with the current dance crazes, but I was. I had just finished choreographing the first year of *Where the Action Is* (1965) for Dick Clark Productions. Jonathan said, "Come with me, Jimmy." As we headed towards the set, he casually said, "I need you to teach Frank Sinatra how to do the swim." In the scene, Frank Sinatra gets into a go-go cage with his daughter, Nancy, who played his daughter in the film, and he does the swim with her. My mind was going crazy! How was I going to teach Mr. Sinatra to dance the swim? Then it came to me. My ballet master, Nico Charisse, taught me well. His words rang in my head. He would always say, "There are a million different ways to get from A to

B." Everyone learns and digests information differently. To teach a dance step to a primarily non-dancer, find some movement like the dance that the person can relate to in his or her real life. Gradually move them into doing the dance, with moves like the dance. It made such sense. I knew that Mr. Sinatra was a fan of boxing, so I had him start with doing an ultra slow speed punching bag movement to rhythm. Gradually, I had him open his hands and turn them upright, continuing the movement. Finally, I had him do the same movement, reaching out sideways. Suddenly, Mr. Sinatra was doing the swim! He was not that secure, so I stood next to Deborah Kerr and Dean Martin during the shot, looking up at him in the cage. He could see me as I did the dance moves and he followed along. It worked. I also taught him a version of the bugaloo, like a dance called the monkey. The director and choreographer were incredibly pleased and, most importantly, Frank Sinatra was happy with me. Nancy Sinatra was ecstatic to be dancing with her dad. I was thrilled.

Frank and Nancy Sinatra in *Marriage On The Rocks,* 1965

Dean Martin, Deborah Kerr, and James Hibbard
in *Marriage On The Rocks,* 1965

Later in the film, we were shooting a sequence that took place at a cantina in Mexico. There were four dancers playing Mexican peasants, and we were dancing behind Caesar Romero and Deborah Kerr. Mr. Sinatra was sitting at a table having some tequila. I am telling this part of the story to demonstrate how supportive and complimentary Frank Sinatra could be but how, in an instant, he could turn on you. He was known for this behaviour. On this occasion, one of the dancers was directly behind him, at camera left. I was next to him, and another two dancers were spaced the same way. Frank Sinatra was well known to have a temper. The dancer who was behind Frank kept screwing up the choreography. After messing up two shots, the assistant director came over to the dancer and told him that Mr. Sinatra was running out of patience. He instructed him to do the choreography correctly on the next shot. I have never seen a dancer so nervous and scared. The choreographer, the other dancers, and I gathered around him and ran through the dance sequence two or three times. We shot it again and, unbelievably, the dancer goofs the shot. Mr. Sinatra got up from the table, came back to the dancer and immediately fired him from the movie. This dancer burst into tears and left. We were shocked! Of course, the other dancers and I were scared shitless. It could happen to any of us. They shot the scene, and everything went well. I was terribly upset that the dancer was treated that way. The choreographer could have repositioned us and put the dancer on the opposite side. It just was not necessary, but that was how Frank Sinatra could be.

James Hibbard, Frank Sinatra, Deborah Kerr, and Caesar Romero in *Marriage On The Rocks*, 1965

Movin' With Nancy Logo, 1967

Movin' With Nancy (1967)

Director and Producer - Jack Haley Jr.

Writer- Tom Mankiewicz

Executive Producer - Nancy Sinatra - Boots Enterprises, NBC Studios

Sponsored by Royal Crown Cola

Broadcast on NBC December 11, 1967

Guest stars - Frank Sinatra, Dean Martin, Sammy Davis Jr., and Lee Hazelwood

The director, Jack Haley Jr., won the Primetime Emmy award for Directorial Achievement in a Music or Variety. The choreographer, David Winters, garnered a Prime-Time Emmy nomination for Special Classification of Individual Achievement for Choreography.

David Winters hired Pete Menefee, ten other male and female dancers, and me to dance on Nancy's special. We danced alongside David, who also choreographed the special. One of the musical numbers was shot out in San Fernando Valley. The song was "Up-Up and Away", a hit song from The 5th Dimension. We had a beautiful hot air balloon. Nancy was inside the balloon, singing, and we were on the ground, dancing. She was lifted high into the air. The hot air balloon pilot and a cameraman were inside the balloon with Nancy, filming close ups of her and shooting us on the ground. We could not see them, as they were crouched down around her knees. On this day, they shot several slow-motion shots of us doing tricks on a trampoline. We would bounce extremely high up into the camera frame. The trampoline was never seen in the filming. It was remarkably effective but, little did we know, very dangerous. On a break, the nurse on set was just bouncing a little on the trampoline and suddenly fell. She started screaming. She had broken her ankle. We picked her up and carried her to a truck for transportation to the hospital. We were all in a state of shock. There was no more fooling around on the trampoline after that.

James Hibbard in *Movin' With Nancy*, 1967

Movin' With Nancy logo, 1967

Nancy Sinatra in *Movin' With Nancy*, 1967

Dancing with David Winters was incredible. David's choreography in this special earned him a special Emmy nomination for his work. David was featured in the dance number "Who Will Buy." It was a high energy number, sung by Nancy Sinatra. David hired twelve of us dancers to join him. It was an extreme honour to be chosen to dance with him, because you had to be at the top of your game. You could not hold anything back, which was what every good dancer longed for.

When you danced along side David Winters you needed to be ready to give your all, or you would disappear. David was electric when he danced. We shot the number on the grounds of the Ocean Park amusement park, while it was closed. In one segment, David asked Pete Menefee and me to dance with him. Halfway through the number, we started a dance segment up on a ledge. We were forty feet up from the concrete floor. The ledge was fifteen feet wide and only five feet deep. It was extremely dangerous. We had no safety wires or nets if we fell off. It was challenging work, with turns, attitude jumps, and tricky footwork. At first, the crane camera was close and at our level, then it would slowly pan back to reveal how high up the wall we were. It made us catch our breath. As the number progressed, the other dancers gradually joined us, down on the boardwalk, for an exciting finish. Those were magical times in all our careers. All of it was provided for us by David Winters. Working with David Winters was an honour. It meant that you were at the top of your game. Magic!

I should add a note about *Movin' With Nancy* (1967). It was ahead of its time by about fifteen years. A number of new things were introduced, including filming, at different indoor and outdoor locations in California, in fast 16mm film with little dialogue. The hour long special looked more like music video vignettes ala MTV.

Chapter Thirteen

Thoroughly Modern Millie

Thoroughly Modern Millie (1967) was one of my most favourite dance jobs. I loved the movie and never got tired of watching it. I have to say, it was an immense pleasure to work with the best dancers in Hollywood, such as Rini Jarmon, Jim Hutchison, Anita Mann, and Buddy Schwab, and stars James Fox, Julie Andrews, Mary Tyler Moore, Bea Lillie, and Jack Soo. It was a real coup to be cast in this movie. The audition was a true Hollywood audition. Every dancer in the country was there. It was a long-drawn-out audition, with hundreds of dancers present. I was one of the lucky ones to be chosen.

One day, I was on my way to rehearsal at Universal Studios and I was running seriously late, having been caught on a gridlocked freeway. I arrived at the studio about forty-five minutes late. I parked my car and ran full speed to the rehearsal soundstage. I came in and all the dancers were lined up facing the director, George Roy Hill, the choreographer, Joe Leighton, the producer, Ross Hunter, and the costume designer, Jean Louis. I was winded from running so far. I looked dishevelled, and was apologetic, as I gasped for air. I ran to the end of the line and said, "I'm so sorry. I was caught on the freeway." All the dancers stared at me. I was so embarrassed. There was a moment of complete silence and suddenly, Joe Leighton said, "You're the one! You will be the Jewish Groom." This was a coveted featured dance role. If looks could kill, I would have dropped dead right there from the glares of the other dancers. Everyone else had been on time, and production was choosing many of the featured character dance roles in the film. I do not recommend being late at any time, but it sure paid off this one time.

Rabbi and James Hibbard in *Thoroughly Modern Millie*, 1967

Julie Andrews, James Hibbard, and Dancers in
Thoroughly Modern Millie, 1967

During rehearsals, the dancers would go to lunch together at the commissary. We were surprised to find that Mary Tyler Moore and Carol Channing would join us many times for lunch. We all fell in love with Mary Tyler Moore and Carol Channing. Once, Carol was sitting next to me. She had a large tote bag with her, and she opened it on the floor. She brought two jars of green liquid out of her bag and placed them on the table. I asked what they were, and she said, "Here, smell this." It smelled like my Uncle Pete Grosso's pasture. She laughed and told me it was the newest rage. It was a healthy mix of pureed greens. None of us had heard of it. She was the first person I had heard of who was into healthy drinks like this. Her bag was still open, and I noticed at least two blond wigs in it. She saw that I was looking and said, "Jimmy, you know, you never know when you're going to need a fresh wig." We all howled with laughter. Mary and Carol were so genuine, and they made us feel relaxed. They were humble and immensely talented. The over-whelming message was, no matter who you are or what you do, be humble and kind. I have never forgotten this. Here were two famous gypsies who have never forgotten where they came from or what it took to get where they were.

Rini Jarmon, James Hibbard, and Julie Andrews
in *Thoroughly Modern Millie*, 1967

All the dancers in the film were at the top of their game. We were working with some the biggest stars in the business, both in front and behind the cameras. It was like a perfect storm. Everything was as good as it could get. I was in show business heaven!

Chapter Fourteen

Fred Astaire and Finian's Rainbow

Finian's Rainbow poster 1968

Finian's Rainbow (1968) starred Fred Astaire, Petula Clark, and Tommy Steele. Francis Ford Coppola directed, Joseph Landon produced, Hermes Pan was the original choreographer, and Claude Thompson was the final choreographer. The film was distributed by Warner Bros - Seven Arts. *Finian's Rainbow* (1968) was nominated for two Academy Awards, five Golden Globes, and a Writers Guild of America award.

Finian's Rainbow (1968) tells the story of an Irishman, Fred Astaire, and his daughter, Petula Clark, who stole a magical pot of gold from a leprechaun and left for America. They arrived in Rainbow Valley, where they became involved in the lives of the locals. Filming took place on the back lot at Warner Bros., where Rainbow Valley was created on nine acres of land.

All of us dancers were over the moon excited about the possibility of dancing with Fred Astaire. Unfortunately, it was not to be. We did have a scene as townsfolk, adlib dancing at the wedding, but our "Burning of the Barn" dance sequence did not include Mr. Astaire. I would have loved to have danced in a scene with Fred Astaire, but I will just have to be satisfied to have been in a film with him. I am, by the way!

We were equally as excited to have the opportunity to work the with legendary Hermes Pan, Fred Astaire's personal choreographer. We began to rehearse with Mr. Pan but, after just the second day of rehearsal, we were greeted by the producer who told us Mr. Pan was no longer going to work with us. Mr. Pan had to excuse himself due to a family emergency. He was to be replaced by Claude Thompson, premiere danseur with the Alvin Ailey Dance Company. We were shocked but thrilled to have a chance to work with Mr. Thompson. We immediately began to work on the "Burning of the Barn" sequence. The dancing was exceedingly difficult. Our characters were townspeople, who were volunteer members of the fire department for the town. Claude chose five of us to do some featured dancing as firemen on the top of the barn. We were dressed in full gear, including boots, coats, helmets, and axes. The gear must have weighed about thirty-five pounds in total. Our choreography included climbing tall ladders to the top of the barn, doing full attitude turns, jumping, chopping with the axes, and dropping to our knees and raising up again, all in a five-person, trapezoid arrangement. We rehearsed for two weeks, on a soundstage dance floor, before heading out to the back lot at Warner Bros. studios for the first time. The barn was about four stories high. The set designer had created a platform, which was about twenty-five feet long by ten feet deep. It was positioned right at the apex of the barn roof, which was about forty feet high. We all went up to the platform by ladders and a crane. The little floor was solidly placed, but there were no safety measures in place to keep us from falling to our death. There were holes in the barn roof, with no nets underneath to catch us if we lost our balance doing the difficult dance combinations. We all said that we needed some safety measures, such as wires or nets. We requested extra danger money to perform on the barn roof. They said they understood and told us to go back to the rehearsal hall. They said they would fix the problem and call us back in a couple of days.

A few days later, they called us back to the set to inspect the safety improvements. Three of us went up onto the platform, at the top of the barn, and we were amazed at what they had done. There were no plans for wires, nets, or anything that resembled safety. They had built another platform of the same size and had mounted it a foot lower, just behind the platform we were to dance on. They said that if we fell, we would just fall backwards on to the extra platform. We looked at them with disbelief. We could not choose where to fall if we happened to fall. We climbed down and all the dancers discussed the options. We decided that if we all stuck together, our safety demands and danger pay would come. We all agreed. We chose one of our five to be our spokesperson and told the producers what we wanted. As we were awaiting their response, Bert May, one of the most legendary dancers in the business, said that he would climb up again and test it once more. We watched, with our mouths hanging open, as he went up. He did a double turn with his fireman gear on. He yelled down, "I think it's okay!" As he climbed down the ladder, we all felt that we wanted to kill him. He had betrayed us and sided with the producers. The rest of us still would not back down. The producers told us to go back to rehearsals and that they would contact us with their decision. Their decision was to cut the dance section out of the number entirely but keep the sequence using all of us as firemen. I have never experienced another similar instance in my entire career. You just never know what challenges you might face.

When we finished principal filming, Francis Ford Coppola, and the producers, threw the cast and crew a wrap party on the back lot. We were having a wonderful time, dancing like crazy, and letting off steam. Francis Ford Coppola, who had been watching me dance the current dances of the time, came up to me and gave me his card. He asked me to call him. I did so, the next day, and he asked me to teach him, his wife, and two other couples how to do the dances. The two other couples were Ed Feldman and his wife, and Phil Feldman and his wife. Both men were renowned producers. Ed Feldman produced the television series *Hogan's Heroes* (1965), and Phil Feldman produced the film *The Wild Bunch* (1969). I met with them at Francis Ford Coppola's house several times and taught them how to do the current dances. At the last dance lesson, Phil Feldman asked if my wife and I would like to attend a studio screening of *The Wild Bunch* (1969). A studio screening is shown only to the cast, crew, producers, PR folks, and friends on the inside, before the film is released to the public. I was flattered beyond comprehension. Charlene and I attended the screening. There, we met William Holden, Ernest Borgnine, Robert Ryan, Edmond O'Brien, Warren Oates, Ben Johnson, Strother Martin, Bo Hopkins, and Dub Taylor. At one point, while talking with Robert Ryan, he asked me what I had done in *The Wild Bunch* (1969). When I explained that I had not played a part in the movie, but was Francis, Ed, and Phil's dance teacher he looked very puzzled, then broke into waves of laughter. Hah! Boy, did I ever feel lucky! The film was sensational. It was such an exciting experience.

Chapter Fifteen

Hello Dolly

Hello Dolly logo, 1969

When I think about it, it is incredible to believe that 2019 saw the 50th Anniversary of *Hello Dolly* (1969). To me, as with everything, fifty years feels like yesterday, just a blink of an eye in time.

The audition for *Hello Dolly* (1969) was not unlike other auditions for major musicals I have attended. The significant difference was the fact that director Gene Kelly, choreographer Michael Kidd, and assistant choreographer Shelah Hackett were the ones putting us through our paces. Every experienced dancer was there. The audition took at least three and a half hours. Fortunately for me, I was chosen to be one of the skeleton crew. This meant that I was one of only sixteen dancers who would be on the film from start to finish. We were the working dancers in town, and we got most of the jobs available. We all knew and respected each other. After three months of rehearsals, Michael Kidd began adding dancers to the shooting schedule and gradually all of the dancers in town came to work on the film. Some of my best friends, who did not get to work on *Hello Dolly* (1969), were able to work for Bob Fosse on *Sweet Charity* (1969). There was no lack of work in those days. I will tell you my story about Bob Fosse later.

First, I want to tell you a story about Gene Kelly. I was finally going to work with the man who inspired me to dance in the first place. I was in heaven. Working for Gene Kelly was a dream come true. First and foremost, he was a real gentleman and all business. He took a liking to me right away and was very friendly. We were the same height, same weight, were both athletic, and he was my idol. Working with him was everything you could hope for. I revered him. When we did some impromptu tap on the Harmonia Gardens set, it was like a couple of buds getting together. It was very relaxed and so much fun. If we missed a step or two, it was not a big deal. There was always lots of laughter. He gave me a small cameo part in the dancing in the park sequence. After I did it, he said, "Do you mind if I show you what I want you to do?" He then demonstrated, in his best Gene Kelly impersonation! I did not do it exactly how he did it, but it was close, and he loved my imitation of him. For the shoot, he advised me to just think of him and then do it my way. He made me feel special. It was very cool.

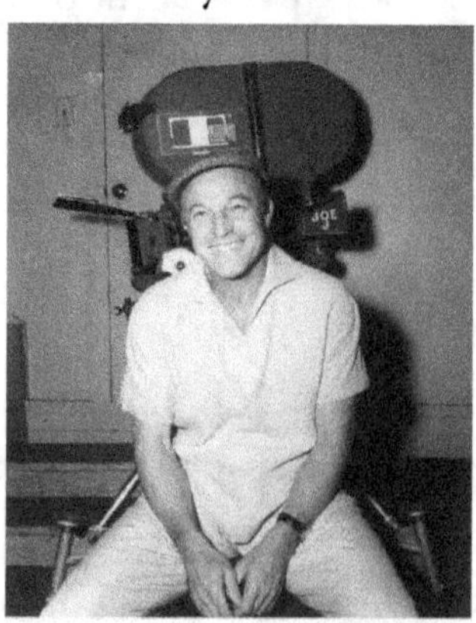

Gene Kelly - Director/Hello Dolly (1969)

Going to work at 20th Century Fox Studios every day was like going to dancer's heaven. We were the elite skeleton crew of one of the biggest movie musicals of all time. When I first started working in films, there were experienced, older dancers who would tell me stories of the films on which they had worked. They would say, "One day, Jimmy, you too will get a long job." Well, fortunately for me, I did get some long jobs, with *Hello Dolly* (1969) being among them.

Every day we had a two-hour ballet bar, led by Shelah Hackett. Shelah was Michael Kidd's assistant choreographer. Michael would come in, usually do a cartwheel, and say, "Let's go." I want to tell you a little about Michael Kidd. Right out of the box, he was wonderful to work for. He was demanding and he knew exactly what he was looking for. When I badly sprained my ankle, in rehearsal, he kept me coming in each day so I would not lose income. The studio wanted to stop paying me until I recovered, but he told them I would be able to learn by watching. He was incredibly supportive. He said, "We dancers have to stick together." I loved him from that moment on.

Barbra Streisand and Michael Kidd in *Hello Dolly,* 1969

The rehearsal regimen of a two-hour ballet bar every morning continued for about three months. When we started to learn the Waiter's Gallop, we all felt that we were in the best shape of our dancing lives. It was so exciting putting that number together. One of the sequences Michael wanted to do was to have some of the boys carry full trays of food, while doing crab-crawls. We jumped at this piece of choreography and tried it, over and over, until Michael was happy with what he saw. Then we moved on to other dance sequences. I said that we felt as though we were in top shape but, the next day, many of us had trouble walking down the stairs. It felt as if chunks of my leg muscles were going to crack, break off, and lie quivering on the floor. I can honestly say, there are various levels of top shape!

After three months of dance rehearsals, the big day finally arrived. It was quite the sight to see Barbra Streisand, Gene Kelly, Michael Kidd, Michael Crawford, Tommy Tune, Danny Lockin, Earnest Lehman, Roger Edens, Harry Stradling, and Irene Sharaff on the rehearsal stage, looking at us. As I mentioned, I had been cast as one of a skeleton crew of sixteen dancers. Our job was to learn every dance number in the film. I was also chosen to be Danny Lockin's dance-in, which meant I had to learn all of Danny's choreography and then teach it to him. Danny's character was Barnaby Tucker. I knew Danny from previous jobs, and he was easy to work with. We began the first day of rehearsals with the principals. No sooner had we started to rehearse, than we were given a break. The break took about forty-five minutes, with Barbra and Gene in a heated discussion. Barbra sat on one of the prop park benches and Gene paced up and down in front of her. Finally, Barbra stood up, hugged Gene, and we resumed rehearsal. There was never a similar episode again. From that moment on, Barbra was the quintessential professional. She was friendly and easy to work with. Sometimes she would ask us to go over a section and sometimes vice versa. I have to tell you; she had the most beautiful skin I had ever seen. It was milky-white, glowing, and flawless. I still can see it in my minds eye.

I have been asked many times about the costumes for *Hello Dolly* (1969), which were amazing. The costume designer was five-time Academy Award and Tony Award winner, Irene Sharaff. Her beautiful designs can also be seen in *An American in Paris* (1951), *West Side Story* (1961), *Cleopatra* (1963), *The King and I* (1956), and *Guys and Dolls* (1955). As dancers, we never saw Irene Sharaff for our fittings. She came to rehearsals in the beginning, when the principals arrived, and she watched the musical numbers as we rehearsed them. She made notes, and never smiled. She made sure that the dancers and the stars could move in her designs, and Gene and Michael would give her suggestions. She was noncommittal about whether she liked the dancing. She was strictly business. At our fittings, her crew knew exactly what she wanted. They made all the changes that ensured we could move in the costumes. The waiter costumes remained tight, to give the right look. Every piece was fitted meticulously to each dancer. When you have the top costume crew you feel as though you have your own personal tailor. In truth, you do. It is not the same with every production but, if the budget allows it, most will hire the best available. *Hello Dolly* (1969) had the best of the best.

Barbara Streisand and James Hibbard in *Hello Dolly,* 1969

We shot the musical sequences for the movie on location in Garrison, New York. We filmed for at least one and a half months on the Hudson River. The church scenes where Dolly marries Horace Vandergelder, were shot on location at the U. S. Military Academy-West Point. This was made possible by pressure from Senator Robert F. Kennedy, just before he was assassinated. The studio made Garrison look like 1890 Yonkers, with new store front names and titles on the train. It was beautiful countryside. We were housed in a hotel in Poughkeepsie, New York, about forty-five minutes away. It was unbearably hot and humid throughout the shoot. Our feet would sink into the asphalt because it was melting. In the photograph, the street resembles yellow brick. It was grey asphalt, painted to look like brick. We had our very own yellow brick road to follow. During this time, there was serious racial tension in the South, Los Angeles, and New York. We were encouraged to stay in the hotel at night. Obviously, if you put a group of dancers together, there will soon be a party. We made sure that staying cooped up in the hotel was going to be fun. In the morning, before leaving for the set, we would core the centres out of watermelon, cantaloups, and other fruit, and fill them with vodka and rum. By the time we returned to our rooms in the evening, the alcohol was completely absorbed into the fruit. Summer fruits are always enjoyable to eat, but our fruit was sensational! It sure helped to pass the time.

Several of the numbers were shot in Garrison, including "Put on Your Sunday Clothes", "Ribbons Down My Back", "It Only Takes a Moment", and "Elegance". While shooting "Put on Your Sunday Clothes", every once in a while, a dancer would faint due to the number of takes and the oppressive heat. There was a new product that the makeup crew had in abundance, called Sea Breeze. It contained alcohol and did the trick in helping to revive the dancers who swooned, and kept the rest of us as cool as possible. It really worked.

Filming *Hello Dolly* Garrison, New York, 1969

During our time in Garrison, we got to know Tommy Tune better. He was such a great guy, friendly, and easy to talk to. Michael Crawford, EJ Peaker, and Joyce Ames were equally as friendly and easygoing. They were lovely. We all respected each other, and we got along famously. Overall, 20th Century Fox made us feel very comfortable. There was something incredibly special about musical show families. Whether on stage or in front of a camera, you were family. You always had each others back and wanted everyone to shine.

On one of our days off, several of us opted to go horseback riding in the morning and would take a Hudson River cruise later that night. When we arrived at the stables, we were asked about our ability to ride and were given a horse that matched our experience. I had ridden a lot in Idaho, when I was younger, so I asked for a spirited mount. Everyone was given a horse before me and, when it came time for me to mount my horse, the foreman pointed to my ride. I was shocked. My horse looked like the swaybacked, drunk horse from the *Cat Ballou* (1965) movie. He was leaning against the fence, looking incredibly sad indeed. I asked, "Are you sure these are spirited horses?" I got on and settled into the saddle. The foreman barely touched the reins and my horse immediately reared up and jumped to life. We slowly followed our leader up a mountain trail until we reached a beautiful, open meadow. Our leader told us that we could now let our horses go. My ride was more than excited. He took off so powerfully that it took me about five seconds to get my head back forward. He was running at full speed within a few seconds, and my horse knew the territory. We jumped two creeks, and he bucked a couple of times. It was the wildest ride I have ever had. On the way back to the stables, the horses knew the way. They started to go faster and went through brush, trying to rub you off their backs. We really had to show them that we had control. It was a great ride.

Later that night, we went on a midnight cruise on the Hudson River. It was one of those booze cruises. I do not know what the captain was doing, except that we got caught on a sand bar and had to wait until early in the morning for the tide to come in and get us floating again. We made it back to our hotel, in Poughkeepsie, just in time to get on the bus to go to Garrison and shoot more of our scenes. Thankfully, we were young and could go all night without sleep and still be ready to start the next day. I cannot do that anymore.

I still remember the first day of shooting the title song, "Hello Dolly," in the Harmonia Gardens set. In fact, it was a day I will never forget. We were taken out of the rehearsal sound stage to see the set. It took my breath away. The set took up almost the entire sound stage. It was stunningly beautiful, and completely practical. We were able to do everything we had been rehearsing for the past three months. With some set designs, there were occasions that some of the dance moves needed to be altered, but the Harmonia Gardens set was perfect. To put the cherry on top of the cake, Barbra Streisand walked in wearing one of Irene Sharaff's designs. We had seen her costume renderings at the rehearsal sound stage, but this was something else. It was a gold gown that she wore for the title song. There was a train attached to the dress. We had to assess whether Barbra could do the choreography with it, and that we could dance near her as we had rehearsed. There was just no way to do it without major changes to the dance. Barbra was tripping on her train, and we could not do the choreography next to her. Irene Sharaff wanted to keep the train on, but both Barbra and Michael Kidd refused. Barbra left and, the next time we saw her, the train was gone. Ms. Sharaff finally relented. I have mentioned this before, and I will say it again. Barbra had the most beautiful skin I had ever seen. She was stunning. We truly were the luckiest group of male dancers in the world, and we knew it!

Barbara Streisand and James Hibbard in *Hello Dolly*, 1969

During an unusually long break from shooting, Gene Kelly asked if there were any advanced tap dancers in our group. One of my fellow dancers, Alex Plasschaert, who was also one of my mentors and teachers, picked himself, Jim Bates, Jim Hutchison, and me. Gene had us stand in a straight line and told us that he was going to create a tap challenge He would do the first improvisation, the next dancer in line would do his, then the next, and so on. When it reached the fifth dancer, we would reverse back up the line until it came back to Gene. Then, he would do a different combination and we would have a chance to show our stuff. The tap challenge was on! We all tried to better one another and impress Gene. We did it about four times through, and we were bushed. It was such fun, and an extreme honour to dance with Gene Kelly. This was the man who inspired me to dance in the first place, when I was just eight years old. This was a classic full circle in my life. I think back to it now and it is overwhelming. I was dancing with the one and only Gene Kelly, eighteen years after he inspired me to dance.

I have told you a little about Gene Kelly, Barbra Streisand, and Michael Kidd, but nothing about the great Louis Armstrong. We were all extremely excited the day Louis Armstrong was on set to shoot his cameo sequence with Barbra. It was part of the title song, written especially for them. Louis Armstrong was watching us do the tap challenge and he called me over to him. He said, "Jimmy, you are a great dancer, but you sweat a lot!" I knew this was true. The makeup crew were always patting me down after every shot. Louis asked me why I did not carry a hankie. He said, "I do, when I play my horn. I sweat a lot, too!" I was one of many dancers in the film, and a hankie was not part of the costume but, to this day, I do carry a hankie when I am teaching tap class and performing. It has become a trademark of mine and it all because of Louis Armstrong's suggestion on the set of *Hello Dolly* (1969).

My memories of Walter Matthau are going to make for a noticeably short paragraph. He did not communicate with the dancers at all. He only communicated with the top brass. "That's all folks!"

Louis Armstrong and Barbara Streisand in *Hello Dolly,* 1969

James Hibbard dancing with hankie

I worked on *Hello Dolly* (1969) for ten months. After principal filming was complete, Gene Kelly and Michael Kidd were responsible for bringing me back in to record foley work. Foley work involved recording sounds, such as footsteps, horse's hooves, and the man sweeping the street. As a side note, that man was me in the opening credits of the film. Michael and Gene knew I had rather good timing, which the foley work absolutely required. I knew all the staging. I had not done foley work before, but I felt as if I had been doing it forever. Our work set included three huge screens, three large miked wooden floors, sections of dirt or grass, and other simulated surfaces that we danced on.

One day, the studio told us that we could invite members of our family to come to the Foley stage. My wife, Charlene, and my daughter, Gianna, who was then four years old, came to watch the proceedings. Everything was going smoothly. Five dancers and I were in the middle of recording sounds from the street sequences, when my daughter decided to sing at the top of her lungs. This display of joy ruined an awfully expensive recording of that sequence. Needless to say, Charlene was asked to take our daughter out of the recording studio, much to my embarrassment. Inviting children and family members to enjoy the process ended that day. I could not have been more embarrassed at the time, but I laugh about it now.

I saw Gene two years after my work on *Hello Dolly* (1969) ended. One day, I happened to be dancing on a segment of the *Dean Martin Show* (1965). As I walked into the hallway, at NBC studios, I heard my name called. The person calling was none other than Gene Kelly. He came over and told me how much he liked my choreographic work with Peggy Fleming on the *Peggy Fleming at Sun Valley* (1971) television show. He thought that it was inventive, creative, and very clever. I could have dropped dead a happy man right then and there. I am telling this story to highlight Gene's well-known reputation of generosity and his support of dancers. He was a major mentor. He was known for remembering names of people and, in this case, that name was mine! It was one of those moments we all need. Someone that you respect, and honour, becomes one of your angels and tells you that you are on the right track. That was what Gene Kelly did for me on that day. It was a magical moment that I will never forget!

I forgot to mention that my voice was on the soundtrack for the *Hello Dolly* (1969) movie. Those of us who could sing had our voices added to the title song. If you listen carefully, you just might hear me. When I think back on that time, I truly was blessed. I was working with the best of the best. Collaborating with people I respected and admired, doing work that turned out to be timeless. *Hello Dolly* (1969) holds such a special place in my heart and memory, and I am forever thankful that I was part of such a great movie. I still have a few more interesting stories to tell you.

Chapter Sixteen

Bob Fosse

Bob Fosse - Director/All That Jazz (1979)

Let me tell you my Bob Fosse story. While working on *Hello Dolly* (1969), I received a call from Universal Studios to audition for Bob Fosse, for the film *Sweet Charity* (1969). I happened to be home sick, with the flu, at that time. I did not want to miss the opportunity to meet and dance for another of my idols. I knew that I would not be available to dance in the film, but it was important for me not to miss the chance to dance for him. A lot of my dance friends and I auditioned for jobs we knew we were not right or available for, because it was important to be seen. An opportunity may happen, down the road, on another project and they would remember you if you impressed them. I dragged myself out of bed and pulled myself together. I felt rough and was in the throwing up stage of the flu. Fortunately, the audition was on a Saturday. I got to the audition and saw that there were hundreds of dancers there. This was a major audition. After learning combinations, we were broken up into groups of sixteen. I was in group number seven, so had a chance to go to the washroom and throw up before it was my turn to dance. Each time a group danced, Mr. Fosse would weed out the dancers he did not think were right. He would go on to watch the next group, who faced the same process, over and over. I was spending a lot of time in the washroom. The audition was taking hours, as there were so many dancers auditioning. Finally, he weeded us down to the group of dancers he was considering. He then placed me in the front, close to where Suzanne Charney, the lead dancer, would be. By now, Suzanne Charney was required elsewhere and had left. We did the combination over and over, and I could not leave to go to the washroom. I just did my best to maintain. Mr. Fosse walked back and forth, while smoking constantly. He stopped right in front of me and blew smoke in my face. I could not leave, and I was unable to hold it any longer. I looked at him and said, "I'm so sorry." I leaned forward and threw up all over the floor. Some of it hit the front of his loafers. He was so startled. He looked down at his feet, leaned over, and stepped backward out of his shoes. He looked back at me and said, "Go home." These were the only two words he said to me during the entire audition. I was so embarrassed. I apologized, repeatedly, as I was leaving. I do not think anyone else has ever thrown up on Bob Fosse's feet! I thought my career was over because of my impressive audition for Bob Fosse. I mean, I literally gave him all that I could.

I was so relieved to get a call from casting offering me the job, but I was so disappointed at the same time. I also felt a little guilty about having gone to the audition knowing that I could not do it. I hope they understood my reasons. I would have loved to have been able to dance in that movie, but I was already fully booked for *Hello Dolly* (1969).

Bob Fosse and Shirley MacLaine rehearsing Sweet Charity (1969)

Chapter Seventeen

Peggy Fleming

Peggy Fleming TV Guide cover

First, I must backtrack a bit to bring you up to date as to how this project came to land in my lap. I met Dick Foster while dancing in *Gypsy* (1962). He was a good dancer, and we became the best of friends. Dick was always moving and shaking with different business ideas. He was a promoter from start to finish. One of our projects was to promote singers by going to record stores and selling forty-five speed records of new recording artists. I do not remember where he got the records, but he was connected to someone. Dick was a born producer. We had crazy fun for a couple of years. Then we went our separate ways.

Years later, in the fall of 1970, I got a phone call from Dick asking me to come to Bob Banner Productions offices. He had a project in mind for me. Bob Banner Productions flagship show was *The Carol Burnett Show* (1967). I was so flattered that he had thought of me. I met Dick at the elevator, and he promptly told me that he was producing a television special for Peggy Fleming. Bob Banner Productions had been the producer for all the Peggy Fleming television specials. Dick had been working for them, for six years, learning the ropes of producing. He said that he had been following my progress for some time and thought I would be right for the project. The guest stars would be Olympic gold medals winner Jean-Claude Killy, singing sensations, The Carpenters, and comics, Pete Barbutti and Shelley Berman.

The director would be Sterling Johnson and the cinematographer would be Robert E. Collins. The special would be filmed, rather than videotaped, and would be shot in Sun Valley, Idaho, during the winter. Sun Valley Lodge was a world-famous ski resort located in my home state. Dick asked if I would be interested in choreographing two production numbers. He wanted me to come up with an idea of something that Peggy and Jean-Claude could do together, that would combine both ice skating and skiing. Dick also wanted a dance number that Peggy, and two male dancers, would do on the ice. This was a tall order, so we agreed to meet and discuss later.

It was such a wildly intriguing concept. For the first, and only, time in my career I dreamed of the idea of how to put Peggy and Jean-Claude together. I had the idea that everything Peggy and the skaters did on the ice, Jean-Claude and the skiers would do on snow. For the second production number, Peggy would do a jazz piece on ice. Figuring out how the dancers would have traction on the ice was solved by using Hushpuppy golf shoes, with two of the pegs sharpened to a point.

For the ski/skate number, Jean-Claude and two female skiers would wear short, 3.5-foot skis. It was a great idea, but I did not know how to ski. It was time for a crash course. In Los Angeles, you can take lessons in how to do anything you need to do, but there is not a lot of real snow to be found. As a result, I had only two skiing lessons on a plastic chip ski slope before heading to Sun Valley. During the first two days, I was on my own trying to apply what I had learned in Los Angeles. I was doing my best on the bunny slope, but I was struggling by myself. A skier saw me struggling, stopped, and asked what I was doing. I told him that I needed to learn to ski as quickly as I could because I was choreographing a television show. He spent about an hour with me, explaining the rhythm of traversing. I listened to his every word. His approach to skiing made perfect sense. Suddenly, I understood the concept and being a dancer helped immensely. Traversing was just like changing directions, from right to left, on a dance floor. For the remaining days, I skied on every ski run I could at Sun Valley. I started to feel as if I had skied all my life. One thing I knew, for sure, was that I had no choice but to get it down. I knew that I would find a way because, if I did not, I would be going home. I was not prepared to go home. The skier, a stranger, saved my bacon. This angel was a gift from heaven.

The first day of rehearsals, with Jean-Claude and the skiers, took place on the bunny slopes of Bald Mountain. The female skiers were members of the US ski team. I needed to find out if my dream made sense to Jean-Claude. Everyone gathered around, including Dick Foster, Sterling Johnson, Robert E. Collins, Mike Melvoin, and two beautiful, Olympic hopefuls, skiers. Suddenly, way out on the slope, we spotted Jean-Claude running on his short skis, just like you would see birds running on water before taking flight. It looked hysterically funny. Jean-Claude was a blessing. Everything that I asked him to try he mastered easily, and he added so much more. The female skiers were experts and did all that I asked of them, including lifts, skiing through Jean-Claude's legs, spinning 360s, and doing cartwheels over the ski poles. Whatever I suggested, they did with great energy and a sense of humour.

We finished filming with Jean-Claude and the girls, and I began working with Peggy and the skaters. Peggy Fleming was one of the nicest, kindest, people I have ever met. Peggy and the skaters duplicated the skiing moves on the ice surface. The number turned into a challenge, with each special move we created for Jean-Claude duplicated by Peggy. It got increasingly difficult, and it built to a great finish, with Jean-Claude skiing right off the mountain onto the ice surface to join Peggy. They then skated off into the sunset together, arm in arm. We broke new ground with the choreography of which I had dreamed. Afterwards, for a couple of Olympic trials, the skiing tricks we came up with were part of the skiing competition requirements.

After we finished shooting the ski/skate portion, the dance number with Peggy, Bobby Elwart, and me was next on the schedule. At the opening of the number, Peggy was at one end of the Olympic sized ice surface and Bobby and I were at the other end. We ran towards Peggy and went into a dancer's split, rolled over, tucked our feet underneath us, and stood up alongside of her. We must have slid thirty to forty feet with the move that normally, on a dance floor, would travel five feet. Peggy could jazz dance in skates, and we had the Hushpuppy golf shoes giving us traction so that we could turn. The number turned out great. Peggy was an absolute dream to work with. Not only was she a supremely talented beauty to look at, but she was also a beautiful person. Peggy's skating choreographer's name was Bob Paul. Bob was an Olympic medal winner and was both an immense talent and a gentleman. He choreographed all of Peggy's television specials. It was a pleasure to collaborate with him.

Here is how much of a professional Peggy Fleming was. One of her solos was scheduled to shoot in front of Sun Valley Lodge, at midnight, with the full moon overhead. This was the dead of winter, and it was very cold, especially that late at night. There was a beautiful pond, in front of the lodge, where the shoot took place. The production crew, Peggy's choreographer, and the makeup and hair crew were all warmly dressed in parkas, ski pants, gloves, earmuffs, boots, and fur hats. Peggy was dressed in an ultra light, flimsy, chiffon, short skating dress. To this day, I do not know how she did it. It was freezing cold, easily fifteen degrees below zero. Peggy was simply gorgeous and skated and performed like a dream. What a professional she was. Peggy's mom made hot mulled wine for everyone, and we refilled our cups continuously. It was so cold that the hot wine began to freeze in the Styrofoam cups. Peggy soldiered on, never complained, and was sensational. I loved working on this special. *Peggy Fleming at Sun Valley* (1971) aired on NBC on January 24, 1971. The revues were all raves. Thanks to my friend, Dick Foster, who hired me, I was now an established working choreographer in the business. I am forever grateful.

Meeting and working with Peggy, Jean-Claude, The Carpenters, Pete Barbutti, and Shelley Berman could not have been more fun. Dick Foster did a spectacular job producing the special. Sterling Johnson, the director, and Robert E. Collins, the cinematographer, both won Prime Time Emmys for their work on this special. My choreographic work just missed getting nominated for an Emmy. Peggy Fleming's production company, Bob Banner Productions, had thrown all their influence behind Ernie Flatt, the choreographer of Carol Burnett's television series. I was disappointed, but Ernie had done spectacular work on that show for many years. Mr. Flatt did win an Emmy for his choreographic work on Carol's show. This was as close as I would get to an Emmy in my career. I believe that, if I had stayed in Hollywood, there would have been more opportunities arising that I could have taken advantage of.

Chapter Eighteen

Tommy

Poster for *Tommy,* 1972

During the 1960s, more choreographers began to enjoy the talent of an immense pool of talented, Afro-American dancers. I remember the first time that I worked with a black dancer was in Ann-Margret's first act in Las Vegas. In 1968, I first worked for a Black choreographer in the movie *Finian's Rainbow* (1968). His name was Claude Thompson. He was a premiere danseur with Alvin Ailey's spectacular dance company. He replaced Hermes Pan. Later, I worked for Claude Thompson again, on the stage production of the rock opera *Tommy* (1969). He remembered me from *Finian's Rainbow* (1968) and signed me to play the doctor, which was a great compliment. Ted Neely played the starring role. Ted and I were already friends. I once choreographed a promo video of one of his pop hit singles, with six dancers. In 1971, Ted starred in the film *Jesus Christ*

Superstar (1973). He was a great, down to earth, regular guy and an immense talent.

We opened *Tommy* (1969) at the famous Aquarius Theater, in Hollywood, on February 22, 1972. The show ran until March 26, 1972. The Aquarius Theater was formerly known as Earl Carroll's Moulin Rouge. Claude's assistant choreographer was the stunning talent, Michelle Simmons. Also in the show was a brilliant dancer named Jerry Grimes. Jerry was one of the best dancers I have ever seen. We also had a husband-and-wife dance team, Bill, and Jacquie Landrum. I was so impressed with their talent, and they really kept me on my toes. I had to be at my absolute best just to keep up with them. Claude Thompson's contemporary style was big, expansive, and required excellent technique to accomplish. As a dancer, it was a next step up for me. Doing his choreography well meant that you were really doing something great.

Ted Neely and James Hibbard in *Tommy,* 1972

Ted Neely and James Hibbard in *Tommy*, 1972

I do not remember ever feeling prejudiced towards people of colour. I treated everyone with respect. One thing was for sure, I was ignorant about racial injustice. I am acutely aware, now, of their struggles every day. During the run of *Tommy* (1969), on our day off, several of the Black dancers asked if some of the white dancers and I would join them to go to a great dance club. It turned out to be in Watts, a neighbourhood in South Los Angeles with a predominantly black population. We walked into the club, and it felt so strange. The activity in the club suddenly stopped. It was like a scene from a movie. People stopped talking and turned and just looked at us. My girl compatriot and I were the only white people in the club. One of our dancing girls took my arm in hers and put her other arm over the shoulder of the other dancer. Immediately, the people in the club relaxed and accepted us. The club went back to normal. It was a tense moment. We had the most wonderful evening. The folks there were gracious. We danced our hearts out until they closed the doors somewhere around 4:00am in the morning.

I was enjoying playing the doctor' and dancing in the run of *Tommy* (1969). The producer, Brian Avnet, asked if I would like to choreograph his production of *Guys and Dolls* (1950) for the San Diego Civic Light Opera. I told him that I would love to but was unsure how I could do this while I was performing in *Tommy* (1969). He told me not to worry, he was the producer and could swing it. He said he would speak to the director and get clearance for me. I had a reputation of being able to work quickly, and I was exactly what he needed. Our director agreed to have my understudy perform my role while I was away. I had a weekend and one week to choreograph a dance-heavy show. What a challenge. The dancers had already been chosen by the production's first choreographer, who had to leave the project after just ten days of rehearsal.

Cast of *Tommy,* Aquarius Theater, Hollywood, 1972

James Hibbard and cast of *Tommy*, Aquarius Theater, Hollywood, 1972

Whomever the choreographer was, he did not realize what he was going to miss. The stars were John Saxon, playing Sky Masterson, and Eileen Rodgers, who was nominated for an Academy Award. To top it off, this production was to be directed by Jim Burrows, one of the most prolific directors, creators, writers in the business. Jim's father wrote *Guys and Dolls* (1950) for Broadway. Jim Burrows had directed more than a thousand television episodes by 2008. He was known for shows such as *Laverne and Shirley* (1976), *Cheers (1982), Friends* (1994), *The Bob Newhart Show* (1972), *The Big Bang Theory* (2007), and *All In The Family* (1971). It was a supreme honour to work with people such as him. I had an incredibly talented cast. The show was a tremendous success for San Diego, and I was thrilled to have been entrusted to do the job. I had a lot of experience working quickly and efficiently, and this was no exception. After the opening of *Guys and Dolls* (1950), I returned to *Tommy* (1969) and finished the run. What a wild and crazy business!

Aquarius Theater, Hollywood, 1972

I forgot to mention that, during our run of *Tommy* (1969), I got to meet Clint Eastwood. He came to see the show and, unbeknownst to me, was dating one of our female dancers. She introduced me to him, after the show, at the stage door at the back of the theatre. What a treat. Ever since he became a star on the television series *Rawhide* (1959), I had been a huge fan. That year was one of his busiest years, as he was about to star in the film *Dirty Harry* (1971).

Chapter Nineteen

From Hollywood To Vancouver

In 1972, I had just finished playing the doctor in the World Premiere of the Rock Opera *Tommy* (1969). We had enjoyed a sensational run. The day after *Tommy* (1969) closed, I headed out of town in my beautiful, 1965 black Mustang, to join my wife, Charlene, and my children, Gianna and Jason, in Vancouver. Charlene and our children, Gianna, aged six, and Jason, aged one, were visiting Charlene's parents, Gillie and Ermie Brandolini. The plan was to visit with the in-laws for a short holiday, and then return to Los Angeles. One day, we found ourselves talking about the lifestyle in Vancouver, as opposed to that in Los Angeles. While there was constant work in Los Angeles, the air in Vancouver was cleaner, the water was better, there were no guns on the streets, and the schools were much better. Vancouver was a stunningly beautiful city, and it was in the same time zone as Los Angeles. We decided, right then and there, to relocate to Vancouver. I figured that, since I had been getting continuous work in Los Angeles since 1962, I could simply commute to any future jobs there. I returned to Los Angeles, packed up our belongings, closed shop, said goodbye to some friends, and returned to what was to be our new home in Vancouver, British Columbia. Wow, life can sometimes be crazy, eh?

Initially, Vancouver turned out to be a culture shock, work wise. There was no television work, other than a local show produced at CTV. This show had some dancing, but not what I was used to doing. The theatre scene in Vancouver was unknown to me. I was not overly concerned because I was sure that the calls from Hollywood would continue to pour in, as they always had. The decision to raise our children in the Vancouver, Canada, atmosphere was paramount in our minds. In truth, I pulled myself out of the Hollywood network all on my own. Nevertheless, I had a family to support, and needed to find work in Canada.

Charlene's dad, Gillie Brandolini, had a friend who was a conductor on the Canadian Pacific Railway. He asked if I would be interested in working as a switchman. He said the money was great and that he would put in a good word for me. I always had a romantic notion of working on the trains, so I decided to give it a shot. I spent many weeks learning how to help the conductor build the train, car by car. I failed my final exam because I filled in the questions in pencil. That test was about sixty pages long. The old boys laughed as they told me I had to take it over again and use only a ball point pen. I wrote the exam again, in pen, and I passed with flying colours. Right away, I was put to work to help put a train together in Port Moody. The train would go into Vancouver, drop off some cars, add some new ones, and then return to Port Moody. I sat on top of the caboose and rode all the way into Vancouver. When I arrived back in Port Moody, at the end of the first day, I walked into the office and promptly resigned from my position as switchman. Working on the trains was not for me. I had never been so bored in my life. I was thankful for the help dad's friend gave me, and fortunately he understood that a switchman's life was not for me. He recognised that show business was in my blood to stay.

Charlene's father, Gillie, owned a hotel in Gastown, close to downtown Vancouver. It was called the Melbourne Hotel and was on the corner of Main Street and Powell Street. He hired me to work part-time, in the beer parlour, as a waiter. This provided some much-needed income while I continued to look for show business work. Graciously, he allowed me to work in the pub, leave to do show business work, and then return to the pub to continue with my work there. This meant that my income would be secure. What a luxury he provided for me. We lived with Charlene's parents, in their loving home, on Granville Street at 52nd Avenue.

There was no television work of any consequence in Vancouver, but I did not worry. I knew that there would be calls from Hollywood any day. Since the television and movie scene was bleak at this time, I interviewed at the Arts Club Theatre for Bill Millerd, artistic and managing director. I applied to choreograph a production of *Dames at Sea* (1966), a spoof of the Hollywood movie musicals. There were only six roles in this play, and the rest of the cast were all well known Canadian performers. Bill hired me on the spot. I was to choreograph and play the role of Lucky, which was a Gene Kelly type role. Charlene played Joan, a Joan Blondell type role. Jeff Hyslop, Canada's leading song and dance man, played Dick, a Dick Powell type role. Susan Anderson played Ruby, a Ruby Keeler type role. Sam Moses, a singer/actor from Toronto, was to play two roles, Hennessy, the stage manager, and the captain of the ship we were going to sail on. To round out the cast, entertainer Toni Sinclair played Mona the movie star. This was the first Vancouver production I was in. It was a co-production with the Arts Club Theatre and entrepreneur, Barry Kaplan.

We opened at the famous Cave Supper Club, which was run by Ken Stauffer. The club was in downtown Vancouver, on Hornby Street. It was called the Cave because it looked like a real cave. Stalactites hung from the ceiling. The Cave was where famous headliner acts, such as Mitzi Gaynor, Diana Ross and the Supremes, Louis Armstrong, Sonny and Cher, Peggy Lee, Ray Charles, Ella Fitzgerald, and the legendary Josephine Baker would break their acts in before heading on to Las Vegas, Reno, Lake Tahoe, Miami, Europe, and elsewhere. At the Cave, Vancouver got to see the best of the best for more than forty years. It closed its doors in 1981.

One night, during the show, we had a memorable funny experience. I had a romantic singing spot in which I profess my love for Joan. The number occurred just before the intermission, with the scene being a wedding rehearsal on the ship on which we were performing. While singing to Joan, I completely drew a blank and forgot my lyrics. It panicked me so much that I created an unknown language in place of the lyrics. This made Joan laugh so much that she blew her lines. The audience quickly clued in that something was amiss. In the finale of the show, we did the same sequence again but this time we would all be getting married. As luck would have it, I blanked again and sang my ridiculous words once more. It made Joan laugh uncontrollably. This, in turn, made the audience laugh. As we were singing and dancing, with full wedding gowns and Navy uniform dress whites, I noticed something shiny on the floor. It was a puddle of water. I jumped across it, pulled Joan to my knee, and we finished the finale. I noticed that my leg was warm and wet. We took our bows and went backstage. As I checked out my wet leg, Joan began laughing hysterically again. We asked her what she was laughing about. She could hardly talk, but she blurted out that she had peed her pants during the number, because of my goofy words. That was the puddle of water on the floor, and now on my leg. We must have laughed for a good fifteen minutes. To exit the Cave Supper Club, you had to go across the stage and leave out of the front door. As we were crossing the stage, the janitor was already there. He had his bucket and mop and was looking at the ceiling, then at the puddle of water, then back at the ceiling, then at the puddle again. He thought there was a leak in the ceiling. We looked at each other and continued to walk out of the theatre. It may have not been our best decision, but we did not say a word. We have laughed about this for years.

Mitzi Gaynor had secured a contract at the Cave, so we had to move our show to another venue. We finished our run of *Dames at Sea* (1966) at the original Arts Club Theatre on Seymour Street, in downtown Vancouver. The building was originally a gospel house, and it was rumoured to be haunted. During our run there, we expected to see a ghost suddenly appear. It certainly added to the regular excitement of doing a show. It was wild and exciting. Our show was successful in both venues.

This project with the Arts Club began many years of working for Bill Millerd and the Arts Club Theatre, one of Vancouver's most successful theatre companies. This work soon led to new projects with Theatre Under The Stars, Vancouver's open-air theatre in Stanley Park, the Vancouver Playhouse, and CBC Radio and Television Studios. The movie industry was just around the corner.

The irony of all this is that Hollywood never called again. I never went back to do another job in Hollywood after leaving. Thinking back, it was my fault that I did not get any more work from Hollywood. My departure was sudden and impulsive. I told some of my friends I was moving, but I should have called the choreographers, studios, and casting agents and told them what I was doing. If they had known where I was, I am certain they would have called. I take full responsibility for calls and work from Hollywood drying up.

After closing *Dames At Sea* (1966) there was not much television or movie work available, so I plunged into building up my teaching portfolio. One of my dance students was a competitive ice skater, named Gigi Boyd. She suggested that I scout out the skating rinks in Vancouver and teach strength and stretch classes to skaters. It turned out to be a great idea. The professional skating teachers were looking for dance teachers to give such classes. I had worked with Peggy Fleming in Los Angeles, so it was a perfect fit. The first club that I worked at was the North Shore Winter Club. The skating pro who brought me in was Linda Broughman. Her star pupil was Karen Magnusen, Olympic Champion. Before long, she had me teaching flow and arm work rink side. I also worked with Barry and Louise Soper, dance champions for Canada. From there, I started assisting Ms. Broughman in embellishing her choreography. This was at the time that famous skaters such as Toller Cranston, Ron Shaver, and Peggy Fleming were changing the skating world with much more flamboyant choreography. Soon, the competitive skaters' parents were paying me to travel with them to various competitions all over Canada. The skating world was tightly knit and, before long, I was working with pros from other skating rinks in Vancouver, such as Hollyburn Winter Club and Newton Winter Club. Eventually, I had the pleasure of working with Toller Cranston and Ron Shaver for a National Skating Seminar. Once you have worked with competitive skaters you are soon in demand. The theory was that one skater should not have the advantage over another. I travelled a lot, the money was particularly good, and I had great fun working with such brilliant skaters. The infighting between pros, skaters, and parents could get serious and tiring. The best way to manage it was to stay out of it and just do the best work possible. I enjoyed working with competitive ice skaters, but I longed to return to work in television, stage, and screen again.

Pam Rosa + Jim

I had started teaching Jazz at Synergy Dance Studios. This led me to Terpsichore Dance Studio and then to Harbour Dance Centre, my current home base. Harbour Dance Centre was the leading adult drop-in dance studio in Canada. I mention these three schools because they have all been owned jointly by a dancer named Pam Rosa (nee Quick). Pam was one of the most humble, lovely people I have ever known. She is one of the most talented dancers

I have ever worked with. She was always the first dancer I hired on every production for which she was available. I have taught for her for at least 38 years. Not only was she my employer, but she was also one of my dancers. She has performed on almost all my Canadian productions and is a member of my dancer's group, called James Angels. We created this group many years ago on the *Rene Simard Show* (1977), a television series for CBC. She will always be one of my angels. Pam is married, with a beautiful family. Despite having had two hip replacements, she still teaches jazz at her studio. Very impressive! Pam is one of my best lifetime friends. I love her with all my heart. We often get together with our many dancer friends we have worked with over the years. We call it Dancer's Happy Hour. We meet at a restaurant for food, drinks, and uncontrolled great fun! These are the types of reunions that feed our souls.

Rosanne Hopkins + Jay Brazeau, *Pajama Game -*
TUTS and Rainbow Stage.

In the summer of 1973, I was hired to choreograph my first show, at Theatre Under the Stars, in Stanley Park. It was one of the last remaining open-air theatres in Canada. It was a jewel of a setting, smack dab in the middle of the park. This beautiful, outdoor theatre had over two thousand seats. My first show with this company was *Pajama Game* (1957). One of the stars was singer/actor/dancer, Rosanne Hopkins. We had a great run in Vancouver and took the show to another outdoor theatre in Winnipeg, Manitoba. Both productions were well-received. Rosanne and I remain good friends and stay connected via Facebook. She lives and still performs in Southern California.

I continued to work at my father-in-law's hotel, as a waiter and part time bartender, and taught dance classes at night and weekends. During this time, Charlene's father, Gillie, and her mother, Ermie, loaned us $3,500 to put a down payment on our first home. It was in North Vancouver, in a suburb called Lynn Valley. The complex was called Yorkwood Hills. Our home was a three-level townhouse, with basement and garage. The complex also had a community swimming pool. The asking price was $35,000. Amazing! We bid the asking price and got the house. I sold my beloved 1965 Mustang and bought two Volkswagen Bugs. Charlene's was a brand new 1973 model, and mine was a 1972 model with a sunroof and a powerful Porsche engine.

By this time, I was working full time as a waiter at The Melbourne Hotel. The hotel was in the famous Gastown district and had the old, separated entrances for ladies with escorts, and another one for men. I had never seen anything like this. In those days, women who came into beer parlours alone were considered unsavoury characters. If they came in with a man, they were okay. This seemed like the dark ages to me. Charlene's older brother, Leon, had worked at the hotel for many years. He was the manager of the beer parlour. Working with Leon and Charlene's dad was a wonderful experience. The regular customers were all colourful characters. There was always something happening. It was not dull.

When Charlene's dad was ready to retire, he sold the hotel to two young entrepreneurs, Barry Kaplan, and his partner, Brian MacDonald. Charlene's brothers, Leon and Harry, and I were asked to stay on and run the business. We did, and what a change it was.

Their ideas were radical. They respectfully asked Gillie what his favourite colour and what his favourite number were. Gillie told them his favourite colour was orange and his favourite number was five. They named the new business No5 Orange Street. Up until then, all beer parlours had bright lights and music kept at a low volume. Barry and his partner's plans included mood lighting, loud music, and an atmosphere geared toward young adults. We had an amazing sound booth with two commercial turn tables and a huge record library. We had a professional disc jockey playing the music. No5 Orange Street became the talk of the town. We had line ups around the block. You had trouble getting in. It was the most jumping joint in Vancouver. It was sorely needed and was a huge success. Leon, Harry, and I continued to work in the beer parlour. Leon was manager, Harry was assistant manager and bartender, and I was a waiter. It was crazy busy and always at capacity.

Jim - Baseball

Besides working at No5 Orange Street, I had the immense pleasure of joining Leon and Harry on the hotel's newly formed fastball team. Gillie, Leon, and Harry all had long histories in sports and Leon had once had the opportunity to play professional baseball with the St. Louis Browns. The team was full of very good ball players. Canada had a long, successful history in fastball. I had loved playing baseball in high school, and I jumped at the opportunity to play for the team. We entered many tournaments, and we won several times. I played the outfield. We had a spectacular time.

The Liquor Control Board would regularly come into the hotel, like Nazi soldiers, and demand we turn up our lights and turn down the music. We reluctantly did so, then as soon as they left, we would revert to low lights and loud music. For at least a year, we believed they had the right to force us to do this. After doing some research, along with other clubs, we discovered that it was an archaic law that was no longer in existence. I remember one night they came in and ordered us to turn down the music and turn up the lights. By this time, we not only knew our rights, but we had the paperwork to back us up. They came in like storm troopers. We offered them a drink and told them they could either leave or stay and enjoy the atmosphere. They left with their tails between their legs. The entire club erupted with cheers of joy. Imagine bucking the system like that! Great days ensued at the No5 Orange Street.

Sadly, in 1973, Gillie Brandolini passed away. He was a great man. He had come from nothing and ended up remarkably successful. He was a loving family man with a successful business. He was also one tough cookie. He was honest, hard working, and respected by everyone who met him. He was a renowned street fighter. In those days, it was tough work to run a hotel. We would revel in stories of his pugilistic endeavours with unruly patrons. Gillie Brandolini could knock someone out with either hand, and sometimes did! With Gillie's passing, Ermie, Charlene, Leon, and Harry decided to buy back No5 Orange Street. They were successful with their proposal, and it was soon back in the family again. We all worked there, but times had changed. The uniqueness of loud music and low lights needed an additional boost for business. There was a night club in town called Gary Taylors, which featured exotic dancers. Harry, Leon, and I visited the club and agreed that exotic dancers would work at No5 Orange. It would be the first time for this kind of entertainment at a hotel pub. The year was 1974 and a new era at the hotel began.

Leon and Harry ran the hotel, and I was designated to organize and run the entertainment. We began with one girl, named Peaches, and soon increased that to three. The dance platform was against a wall and the dancers entered through the house. This was a city bylaw violation, and my show business sensibilities told me that this was wrong. We decided that it was time to renovate. We moved the dance platform to the center of the beer parlour and, for the dancers to get to the stage without coming through the house, we cut a hole in the ceiling. This led to a linen closet, directly above the stage. Charlene and I designed a ladder, made of high-density plastic, with the strength of a regular workman's ladder. It was hollow we put Tivoli twinkling lights inside. The dancers would climb down the ladder to the stage without coming through the house. It provided some mystery, as well as safety from offhand remarks from sloppy customers. It looked classy and worked perfectly. Soon, we had girls coming in who were new to the profession. They felt safe at the No5. I worked with them, choreographing and developing the best dancers in town. We had nonstop dancer entertainment each day. Initially, working with the dancers was fun. Most of them were easy to work with but, as the number of girls increased, it became a real job. Some of the girls had a great professional attitude, but most did not, and it became hard to deal with them.

In 1976, US production companies began coming to Vancouver to enjoy the monetary exchange. My luck changed when *The*

Wolfman Jack (1976) television show came to the CBC. Wolfman Jack was a famous Los Angeles radio disc jockey personality. Two of the No5 Orange dancers, Jackie Coleman and Shirley Kozak, were professional dancers and were hired to dance on the series. They mentioned my name to the choreographer, Andre Tayir. What luck! Andre was a good friend of mine from Los Angeles. As soon as Jackie and Shirley told him that I was living in Vancouver, he called and asked if I would be interested in assisting him on the series. I had to find a replacement to run the show at No5 Orange. Fortunately for me, my beautiful wife saved my bacon. Charlene agreed to take over at No5 Orange, so that I could work on the show. This signalled the end of my days working at No5. Once I began working for the CBC, a continuous stream of projects opened up. I was back working in television and on stage. My angels were looking out for me. I assisted Andre Tayir with the choreography and was one of the dancers on the show. Andre had to leave because of health reasons, and I finished choreographing the remaining episodes. From that moment on, I never looked back. Work in television was opening up and I was again in the right place at the right time and loving it! A new era in the Vancouver television and film business was born.

The Wolfman Jack (1976) show was the beginning of Hollywood North in Vancouver. To my knowledge, it was the first US/Canada co-production on the west coast. It was the one of the first US productions to shoot in Vancouver, taking advantage of the dollar exchange. It started the flood of business from the US and was a perfect marriage. Canadian camera operators, costume designers, set designers, producers, directors, and talent were ready to work as fast and as proficiently as artists in the United States.

My next project at the CBC was choreographing *The Rene Simard Show* (1977). It was produced and written by Alan Thicke. He appreciated my work on the *Wolfman Jack* (1976) and my reputation and history in Los Angeles. Alan hired me to choreograph both the first and second years of the show. My dancers were billed as James Angels, and included Valerie Easton, Viktoria Langton, Jackie Coleman, Shirley Kozak, and Pamela Quick. I still wear a gold angel, on a gold chain, which represents my James Angels.

In between, I was able to sandwich in choreographing Ann Murray's *Ladies Night* (1978) television special at the CBC facilities in Toronto. I also choreographed television specials for producer Ken Gibson, at the CBC. Every week my dancers would feature in a production number. My lead dancer was Jeffrey Hyslop, world renowned singer/dancer. Working with Jeffrey was a dream come true. He was immensely gifted. He had performed, all over the world, in television, movies, and on Broadway. We quickly became lifelong friends. I worked with Robbie Rae, who has since passed away, and Cherrill Rae, who I am friends with on Facebook. We communicate frequently. She has remarried and lives in Miami, Florida. She still sings and performs regularly. She recently was inducted into the London Rock and Roll Hall of Fame.

I choreographed several episodes of *Canadian Express* (1977) for CBC, with producer Patsy McDonald. I was able to feature my dancers on that show, too. In 1979, Ken Gibson hired me again to choreograph a CBC television special for Country Western Hall of Fame singer, Carroll Baker. I was so busy at that time. Back in Vancouver, I was hired to dance on the *Gospel And Minister Candyman* (1984) television special, starring legendary singer Leon Bibb. The choreographer was the great Michelle Simmons, whom I had worked with in Hollywood. It was an honour dancing on this special, especially as my assistant choreographer, Mary Lou Brien, and I were the only Caucasian dancers on the show. That was an incredibly special compliment to Mary Lou and me. The choreography was extremely difficult, exciting, technical work.

Patsy MacDonald + Jim

Mike Watt and friend

Let me take this moment to talk about Mary Lou Brien. Mary Lou was a wonderful dancer. She was exceptional at every discipline, including jazz, musical theatre, and tap. She reminded me of Gwen Verdon, of Broadway/Bob Fosse fame. She was a great assistant for me. She picked up instantly and never forgot any staging I dreamt up. She kept me grounded. Her personality was always bubbly and positive. I love her dearly. We did a great deal of work together in both television and on stage. At any given time, I could feature her, knowing she would come through and be wonderful. She was such a bright light. She went on to a successful career as a director and choreographer in her own right. She was and is extraordinary.

Mary Lou Brien + Jim

The most rewarding experience I have had with choreographing all these years is the opportunity to put dancers to work. Dancers do not often get steady work in this business, but I was fortunate to have all the work I could manage. Consequently, I could give work to many dancers on a steady schedule. It was crazy and won-derful. Some of the superlative dancers who worked for me have gone on to spectacular careers of dancing, acting, choreographing, directing, and producing. This included Mary Lou Brien, Pamela Rosa (nee Quick), Valerie Easton, Viktoria Langton, Teryl Rothery, Max Reimer, Mary Lou Brien, Jeff Hyslop, Carol Murphy, Christine Chipperfield, Wendy Abbott, Sandi Croft, Kim Breiland, Marlowe

Windsor, Susan Lehman, Jamie Zagoudakis, Shelley Stewart Hunt, Tamara Thompson Levi, Belinda Sobie, Catherine Leighton, Jerry Pender, Lovena Fox, Carol Murphy, Barbara Tutt, and Marlowe Windsor. There are so many more, too numerous to mention. I love and honour every one of them.

Each summer, the Arts Club Theatre of Vancouver produced a major musical at the main stage on Granville Island. For dancers it was the highlight of the year. For me, it gave me my first opportunity to stage a musical originally directed and choreographed by Bob Fosse. He was an idol of mine. I loved his style and I related to how he communicated through song and dance. The show, *Pippin* (1972), starred Canada's premiere song and dance man, Jeff Hyslop, as Pippin, my wife, Charlene Brandolini, as the Queen Mother, Kim Hall as the Leading Player, and dancers Mary Lou Brien, Catherine Leighton, Viktoria Langton, Jerry Pender, Max Reimer, and Teryl Rothery. Our production was highly successful for the Arts Club!

Pippin line of dancers, Pippin - Arts Club theatre

Later that year, I choreographed a fitness series titled *In Motion* (1980), produced by Michael Liebowitz, and starring my top dancers. The series could show an entire five-minute segment, or as little as fifteen seconds between the end of one television program, and the beginning of the next. This was called interstitial segments. It was great fun, because it combined regular fitness exercises with dance, which was quite unique for the time. From that, I worked on a commercial for Super Socco, one of the earliest sports power drinks. We had fourteen dancers on this well-funded commercial.

1980 brought me back to the Arts Club to choreograph the clever revue musical *Starting Here, Starting Now* (1976), with lyrics by Richard Maltby and music by David Shire. Our production starred my wife, Charlene Brandolini, Kim Stebner, and two Toronto imports. We played the Arts Club Revue stage, on Granville Island, and went on tour to the Belfry theatre in Victoria, BC. This production captured the attention of the extremely successful Stage West Dinner Theatre in Edmonton and Calgary, Alberta. Their policy was to cast famous movie and television stars in their dinner theatre musicals and revues. They contracted me to direct and choreograph *Starting Here, Starting Now* (1976), starring George Chakiris and my wife, Charlene Brandolini. George Chakiris was a beautiful, gentle, soul, with a great singing voice, and a truckload of talent. His partner was an artist who did charcoal paintings of Charlene and my son, Jason, and gave them to us as a gift on closing night. They were wonderful. They hang in our media room. George currently lives in Los Angeles and has a successful business designing gorgeous jewelry.

George Chakiris + Charlene, *Starting Here Starting Now*,
Stage West (Calgary and Edmonton)

More American producers were coming to Vancouver. In 1980, two producers, Clancy Grass and Burt Rosen, came up to shoot the *Tom Jones* (1980) television series at the Panorama Studios in West Vancouver. I knew Burt Rosen from Hollywood. He was half of Winters/Rosen Productions, whom I had worked with on several productions. Clancy and Burt hired me to choreograph the series.

I had four statuesque, beautiful dancers on the show. They were Viktoria Langton, Candy Moroz, Teryl Rothery, and Debbie Wakeham. Meeting and getting to know Tom Jones was a real treat. He was a guy's guy. He liked smoking a cigar, drinking champagne, and telling jokes. He was down to earth, fun to be around, and easy to work with. He was a little like Elvis Presley, he would try anything and then do it in his style. My job was simply to give him moves with which he was comfortable. He did everything well and was completely professional. Tom had a reputation that preceded him, and, in our case, he did not let anyone down. He had a reputation with women that was Hollywood legend. Believe me, he has earned it! On our first day with Tom, the producers, crew, and dancers, were having a meet and greet. It was great fun meeting everyone. Tom wanted to meet the dancers, so he introduced himself to them one by one. When he got to the fourth and last girl, eighteen-year-old Candy Moroz, who was drop dead gorgeous, he asked her name and age. When she gave her age, Tom took her by the hand, walked her out of the rehearsal hall, and called lunch! We were stunned. His bad boy reputation was very much intact. Tom Jones was, and is, a powerhouse performer. On his show I got to choreograph him, the great Hal Linden, and the wonderful Dionne Warwick, just to name a couple.

A heart-warming experience with Tom Jones is worthy of telling. One night, I brought Charlene's grandmother, Filomena, to the taping of an episode. She was 98 years young and was a huge fan of Tom's. She spoke in broken Italian and called him Tommy Johnson.

I told the director about her and showed him where she was sitting. During Tom's opening up-tempo song, the director had one of the cameramen aim his camera right on Charlene's Noni. She was fanning herself with the program and, at the end of the number, she took a big breath and exhaled. She looked as though she was completely overheated, and she probably was! It was so funny, and everyone laughed. Tom introduced himself to her. It was spectacular! Her cheeks were flushed with pink! It was one of the few times I had ever seen her smile.

I later had the pleasure of choreographing the film *By Design* (1981), directed by Claude Jutra, and starring Patty Duke (Astin), and Canadian star, Sara Botsford. I choreographed and played the role of Carl. It was great fun to work with Patty Duke. She was very funny, friendly, and down to earth. She was powerful on screen, and you could not take your eyes off her.

In 1982, the CBC hired me to choreograph two episodes of *The Paul Anka Show* (1982). We did two big production numbers, starring Paul Anka and featuring some of the best dancers in Canada, including Pamela Rosa (nee Quick), owner of Harbour Dance Centre, and Belinda Sobie. They were both startlingly beautiful dancers. I was also hired to choreograph a production of *The Pajama Game* (1957) for one of the few outdoor theatres in North America, the Rainbow Stage, in Winnipeg, Manitoba. This production starred the wonderful Canadian triple threat, Wanda Cannon, one of Canada's leading actors, Jay Brazeau, and Vancouver's own, Rozanne Hopkins. Rozanne reprised the role of Gwen Verdon, that she had performed for Theatre Under The Stars in Vancouver. I really enjoyed the experience in Winnipeg. Rainbow Stage was located next to the river, and the mosquitos were the biggest and most aggressive I had ever seen. They would literally fly into the actors' mouths when they were singing! Yowzah!

James Angels - L to R- Belinda Sobie, Laurie Briscoe, Pam Rosa, Viktoria Langton, Wendy Abbot, and Mary Lou Brien (Paul Anka tv series)

In the summer of 1983, I was back at the Arts Club Theatre, on Granville Island, to choreograph a production of Bob Fosse's *Cabaret (1972)*. This was a dream come true for me. I had idolized Bob Fosse, but never got to work with him. Finally, I had the opportunity to present the second of his acclaimed shows for Vancouver audiences. I loved his style of choreography, and it was amazingly comfortable for me to stage the show. We had one of Vancouver's star singer/actors, Jane Mortifee, as Sally Bowles, the sensational Simon Webb as the MC, and some of Vancouver's best dancers and singers. It was a great production and was held over three times past its original run. At the same time, I had the opportunity to choreograph *Godspell* (1973), at the Vancouver Playhouse, and to become the entertainment director of a brand-new nightclub, Confetti, owned by restauranteur Bud Kanke. *Godspell* (1973) was directed by one of

Canada's leading directors, Walter Learning. I welcomed the opportunity to work with him. Our production starred Canadian singer/actors Morris Panych, Sam Mancuso, Lelani Marrell, Susan Skemp, who is now my business partner, and Moira Walley, who has gone on to become head writer on the spectacular tv series *Breaking Bad* (2008), winning an Emmy for her writing.

Confetti, a trendy nightclub with a New Year's Eve theme every night, proved to be a 24/7 job. It was very taxing. In that business, you do not turn down work if possible. In this case, I decided to do both projects at the same time. Each project would prove to be exhausting enough by itself. I would rehearse *Godspell* (1973) all day, then run to Confetti and work until the wee hours of the morning. Just before opening night for both projects, I was on my way home just outside of Horseshoe Bay. The last thing I remember, before waking up, was how good I felt driving with all the windows down and the freshness of the cool night air. I woke up after crashing my car into the side of the mountain. My body just gave out. I was so tired. This was a reality check. I am not Superman, even though I thought I could go on and on without getting enough rest. If I had not been driving my 1972 Mercedes, I would not be here today. The entire car was totally crushed, except for the driver's compartment. I was hurt, with broken bones in each wrist, a broken nose, severe body bruises, and a sprained neck. Thankfully, I was alive. I was in shock as I got out of the car and made my way up the embankment to the highway.

I tried to flag down someone to help me, but no-one would stop. A truck driver was the only person to stop and help. He helped me into his truck and then called the police for me. I do not remember his name, but he was an angel, nonetheless. I was in Lion's Gate Hospital for three days before being discharged. From this moment on I have taken better care of myself, which is what we should always do. When I went to get my valuables out of my car, I could not believe

I had lived through that. I am so thankful that my little 1972, four door Mercedes was built like a tank and that my angels were there with me.

The summer of 1984 found me, once again, at the Arts Club Theatre to choreograph a production of Abe Burrows *Guys and Dolls* (1955). I had such great fun choreographing that production. It was a blessing to approach it, for the second time, after choreographing it in San Diego in 1977, for Abe's son, director Jim Burrows. Our stars included one of Vancouver's most successful leading men, Winston Rekert, as Sky Masterson, my wife, Charlene Brandolini, as Adelaide, Dean Regan, one of the funniest actors I have ever worked with, as Nathan Detroit, and Marilyn Gann as Sarah Brown. We also had leading character actors, such as Jay Brazeau and Simon Webb in our production. We had the best dancers available. The show was highly successful.

Guys and Dolls Charlene Brandolini, Winston Reekert,
Catherine Leighton, *Guys and Dolls* - Arts Club Theatre

Charlene Brandolini as Adelaide, *Guys and Dolls* - Arts Club Theatre

In 1985, one of Vancouver's leading musicians and band leaders, Bobby Hales, asked me to create a show he was producing for an outdoor venue at the Pacific National Exhibition, which was Vancouver's annual fair. My wife, Charlene, and I wrote, produced, directed, costumed, and choreographed a singing and dancing extravaganza. *With Love, From Canada* (1985) had a cast of twenty of Vancouver's finest artists, including Charlene, Andy Thoma, Dean Regan, and the wonderful Bobby Hales and his orchestra.

A producer, who had a contract from the Canadian Military, saw our show. He hired us, and our show, to travel with the Canadian Military and entertain the Canadian Peace Keeping troops stationed in Germany, Israel, and Cyprus. We added Canadian Rock and Roll inductees Bill Henderson and his band, Chilliwack, and the French chanteuse Veronique Beliveau. We also included a French-Canadian comedian, Vancouver singer/actress, Charlene Brandolini, and singer/actress, Lovena Fox. Our eight beautiful female dancers included Viktoria Langton, Debbie Belton, Marlowe Windsor, Shelley Stewart Hunt, Kim Breiland, Max Reimer and his adagio partner, and me as the song and tap-dancing man. The Canadian Military took care of us as though we were royalty. They escorted us everywhere, for our safety, and gave us the dream of a life tour. In Germany, they took us to the gambling house at Baden Baden, where the movie *Casino Royale* (1967) was filmed. In Israel, they took us to all the historic sites, including Jerusalem and the historical city of Jericho. On one amazing outing, we were taken on the Way of the Cross. It was full of shopping booths and, occasionally, a Bedouin and his camel would walk right by us. It was like stepping back in time. They took us to the Dead Sea, where we had the famous mud baths and swam. It was true that you could not sink in the Dead Sea because of the high salt content. You pop around like a cork. We were taken up Mount Masada, where we saw cave openings where the Dead Sea scrolls were found. On top of Mount Masada there were still the remains of the city built by the Israeli people who had escaped from the Romans. There were remains of their baths, with original-coloured tiles still visible. There were huge cisterns, dug out of the mountain, where they stored water collected from rainfall, which happened rarely. They were an engineering miracle! If you looked down over the edge of the mountain you could still see the outlines of the Roman encampments on the Judean desert floor. Those images stayed in my mind forever.

The Canadian soldiers were the best audience any performer could ever have. You felt as though you could not do enough for them. The tour was in December, leading up to Christmas, so they were yearning to be with their families back home in Canada. It was such a profound experience. I once choreographed the Kim Sisters, for one of Bob Hope's USO tours, but I never travelled with him.

In 1987, I directed and choreographed a production of Cole Porter's *Anything Goes* (1934) for Theatre Under the Stars. This production starred my wife, Charlene, and singer/actor Rex Downey. This production also featured a young ingenue by the name of Susan Skemp. She was a petite, beautiful, blond haired singer actress. She was the quintessential girl next door. After all these years, Susan and I are working together again. She is my editor and assisting me with writing my autobiography. I could not do this without her. Her support is unfailing, and she keeps me running. We also have a couple of other projects we are developing in addition to my book.

During rehearsals for *Anything Goes* (1934), I met Cliff Cox, who was on the Board of Directors of Theatre Under the Stars. Cliff Cox was an opera singer in England when he was younger. Upon moving to Canada, he founded the Hamilton Opera Company before he moved to Vancouver. He was also an engineer and owned a company called DB Equipment Ltd. One day he asked me, "What are you going to do when you grow up?" I laughed and told him I planned to continue to do just what I was doing. We became instant friends. He owned a heating and air conditioning distribution company and had a new product that needed launching in Western Canada. He asked me if I would like to try my hand at marketing, and selling, his product line. He understood that my career in show business was in full gear, but he would be happy if I worked for him when I was not working in show business. When jobs came up, he was willing to let me do them, and then return to his company when the show business work was finished. It could not be a better offer for me. It was at a time when getting a credit card, or a loan for a mortgage, was too difficult for a dancer/choreographer due to the sporadic show business work opportunities. I decided to give it a shot. Little did I know that this would be a job I would hold for twenty-five years. Yes, twenty-five years! My dad loved the fact that his dancer son finally had a legitimate job. I enjoyed working for Cliff. I had always enjoyed learning something new. I ended up having a successful career, marketing and selling heating and air conditioning equipment for him. It provided us a home, cars, savings, and everything else that goes along with a steady income. My show business work did not stop at all. Cliff would allow me to do my gigs and then come back. I owe a lot to Cliff Cox, providing me with the best of both worlds. I continued to work in show business and sell equipment for Cliff at the same time.

In the fall of 1987, the Canadian Military asked us to offer an idea for another show tour. This time, the tour included entertaining the Peace Keeping troops in Germany, Israel, Cyprus, and Egypt. Several producers across Canada sent in their show ideas for adjudication. Luckily for us, our show was chosen for the second time. Cliff Cox was true to his word and gave me his blessing to go. He asked that when I was finished, I come back to his company and continue marketing his products.

Charlene and I produced, wrote, directed, and choreographed this presentation, too. Charlene also designed the costumes. Our headliner act was the great, award winning recording artist Bill Henderson and his band Chilliwack. We also featured Bill Henderson's daughter, singer/dancer Saffron Henderson, singer, Andy Thoma, and singer Charlene Brandolini. Like our first show, we brought in a French chanteuse, Anne Bisson, a French comic, and eight dancers including, Viktoria Langton, Valerie Easton, Shelley Stewart Hunt, Debbie Belton, Marlowe Windsor, and me.

Bill Henderson, Charlene Brandolini + Jim

It was another wonderful tour. Besides performing for soldiers in Germany, Israel, Cyprus, and Egypt, our escorting officers escorted us everywhere, once again. We were all so excited when we returned to the Casino at Baden Baden. We had plenty to drink and got very loud. The Casino manager asked us several time to keep the noise down, but we were seriously partying! I struck up a conversation with a German fellow in one of the many bars. This was odd because he did not speak English and I did not speak German. I was very drunk, and I invited him to come to see the show at the base. Somehow, he understood and showed up at the base the next night to see the show. Crazy, eh!

Once again, we flew to Israel in the Army's Hercules cargo plane. Our gear, and us, were in the belly of this huge plane. It was not comfortable, but it was exciting. Some of us fell asleep in the canvas seats and some of us crawled up on the mountain of gear and fell asleep there. You had to wear ear plugs as the noise was intense. I was invited up into the cockpit to meet our pilot, who turned out to be one of the few female pilots in the Canadian Armed Forces at the time. I was shocked to discover that the floor of the cockpit was glass. You could see straight down. At that very moment we flew over the Matterhorn, which straddles the border between Italy and Switzerland! I mean, right over the top. It was an extraordinary experience! So Freaky!

Our escort officer, Major Wayne Lee, introduced us all to the sights. In Tel Aviv, we had our first dinner on the beach of the Mediterranean Sea. We also visited the Church of the Holy Sepulchre. There were several denominations in this holy place. This was where Jesus was crucified, and it also houses the tomb where he was buried and resurrected. Since biblical times, civilization after civilization was built on top of each other. To get to the Cross, we had to go down three stories. Once there, we had the experience of touching what was considered the base of the cross that Jesus was crucified on. It was a powerful moment. We had mud baths and, once again, swam in the Dead Sea. The Dead Sea was not deep. At the deepest, the water only came up to our chins. As you walk in, it starts cold and all of a sudden gets very warm. Once again, we went up Mount Masada. This time, the men in the company decided to climb it while the rest of the company used the gondola to get to the top. I was the last to reach the summit, exhausted. Andy Thoma treated it like a race. He was in such good physical shape. He ran to the top. He was there long before any of us. It was a gruelling climb. From the top you could see the Dead Sea in the distance. Touring the ancient Jewish city on top was an amazing experience.

From Israel, we flew to Northern El Gorah Air Force base, in the middle of the Egyptian desert. It would be our home base while there. We flew in a French Transall cargo plane, like the Hercules, but smaller. In Southern El Gorah we performed in an ancient amphitheater for the soldiers. Right behind us was the Red Sea. The night was beautiful, hot, and the multitude of soldiers were so happy to see our show. It was all so powerful! On our return to Northern El Gorah, we rode in a bus up the coast to the famous resort Sharm El Sheikh. We stopped there for drinks and stayed a couple of days in Cairo for some RnR. We stayed at the Marriott Hotel, which originally was the palace of King Faroud. It was opulent, plus so beautiful and elegant. When we were taken shopping, we were escorted out of the gates of the hotel and suddenly we were shoulder to shoulder with the people of Cairo. There were millions and millions of people in Cairo. It was so crowded. What a shock! It was a profound dose of reality.

One day, our escort officers took us all into the Kahn shopping area and stayed with us the whole time. We could not go off on our own. Our officers told us it would be too dangerous. While there, we bought gold jewellery, carpets, and some clothing. We visited the Sphinx and the Great Pyramids of Giza. We took a tour inside the Great Pyramid of Giza. The stairs inside were steep, poorly lit, and crowded with people in front and behind, so close you were touching. The air was hot and musty smelling. It took about forty minutes to climb up the stairs to a room near the top. The room contained only an empty tomb, and we were immediately ushered back down the same stairs. We could not wait to get out! It was all so overwhelming! After getting out, we immediately rented some horses and rode around all the pyramids. Finally, there was some fresh air!

We had a scary time returning from Cairo to Northern El Gorah air force base by bus. En-route, we encountered a frightening desert sandstorm. The driver of the bus was familiar with this kind of problem. We would drive for a while, and then the sand would completely cover the highway. We would have to wait until the driver could see some of the road again. Suddenly, you could see about ten feet in front, and there would be a Bedouin and his camel walking along. Then everything would disappear once more. All this took an extraordinarily long time, hours and hours. Saffron, Bill Henderson's daughter, was severely diabetic and had only brought enough insulin for a short bus ride back to the base. By the time we reached the base, Saffron was in diabetic shock. We were all so scared. Saffron was in bad shape and had to stay at the base hospital for three days before she could rejoin us back at the base in Germany. Fortunately, for all of us, she recovered.

Throughout the entire tour we had the profound pleasure to perform for the peace keeping soldiers from Canada and many other countries including Germany, Israel, Cyprus, Austria, and Egypt. These tours took place during Christmas time and the soldiers were lonely, missing their families, and genuinely wanting to go home. They were the best audiences you could ever imagine. They welcomed us with complete open arms. They gave us private dinner parties and were always trying to ferret us to their private digs. One of Canada's elite jet fighter pilots fell in love with one of our dancers, Viktoria Langton. Viktoria had that effect on most men. He secretly flew his jet a couple of times to Vancouver, after the tour, to spend time with her. The Canadian jet flying aces were the elite and never seemed to get into trouble.

Not only did we get to see wonderful sights on the tour, but we will never forget performing for the soldiers involved with peace keeping in Europe and the Middle East. I think about our experiences with the Canadian Military every single day. We were all so blessed to have taken part. I fulfilled my part of my agreement with Cliff Cox and returned to his company and continued to market and sell heating and cooling equipment.

In 1988, I directed and choreographed *Little Shop of Horrors* (1982) for Theatre Under the Stars. I loved doing this show. The book was by Howard Cashman, and the music by Alan Menken. The talking, singing plant, which was one of the stars of the play, grew big enough to totally swallow an adult, right in front of your eyes! The plant operator had to do many things at once, such as mouth the dialogue, lip sync the lyrics, and swallow people at the same time. He was inside the body of the huge plant on stage for most of the show.

The voice actor for the plant sat in the control booth, throughout the show, and performed on a microphone from there. This was the incredibly talented, Duff MacDonald. His magnificent base/baritone voice was extraordinary. Duff is still working constantly on stage, television, movies, and social media. Our production was highly successful. It so impressed the Jessie award jury, that they nominated two stars, Colleen Winton, who played Audrey, and Jamie Cronk, who played Seymour, for Best Actor awards. They also nominated me for my direction and choreography. The Jessie award is our local version of a Tony award on Broadway. In the end, the Jessie award jury had to rescind all the nominations because our production was semi-professional, not fully professional. Still, it was a great compliment.

The following summer, Bill Millerd, Artistic Director for the Arts Club, asked me to remount *Little Shop of Horrors* (1982). This time, the voice of the plant was performed by beloved Canadian actor, Denis Simpson. I was again nominated for Best Direction and

Choreography. I did not win, but my new female star, Lelani Marrel, won the Jessie Best Actor Award for her portrayal of Audrey. This same year, I directed and choreographed a production of *Best Little Whorehouse in Texas* (1978) for Theatre Under the Stars.

Later that year, I had the pleasure of choreographing a production number, for ten dancers, on an episode of the hit television series *MacGyver* (1985). The guest star was the beautiful Teri Hatcher, actress best known for *Desperate Housewives* (2004). She was a trained dancer whom I knew from my days in Hollywood. Since she was an accomplished dancer, we were able to do a lavish Egyptian themed production number with lots of dancing, reminiscent of the musical movies of Hollywood. Teri Hatcher and my dancers were wonderful! I was also given an acting role of the choreographer. Each time I finished my show business jobs, I returned to DB Equipment Ltd. and continued to market and sell equipment for Cliff Cox.

In 1990, I acquired the rights to produce the musical comedy *I Love My Wife* (1977). I took the project to Bill Millerd, Artistic Director of the Arts Club Theatre. It was the perfect show for their summer musical. Bill agreed to produce it. I directed and choreographed the production. *I Love My Wife* (1977) was the stage adaptation of the movie *Bob, Carol, Ted, and Alice* (1969). The stage musical book and lyrics are by Michael Stewart, with music by Cy Coleman. It was very funny.

Our production's two local stars were Norman Browning and my wife, Charlene Brandolini. Norman was one of Canada's leading actors. He resembled a young Art Carney, very funny, and charming. Charlene Brandolini was beautiful, and very funny. Two Toronto singer/actors, Deirdre Van Winkle and Victor Young, rounded out the lead cast of four. We had four musicians, who played acting roles as well as played music on stage with the actors. It was highly successful for the Arts Club Theatre.

In 1991, I was hired by Stage West Dinner Theatre of Edmonton and Calgary, Alberta to direct and choreograph their production of *I*

Love My Wife (1977). One of their representatives had seen our Vancouver production and secured my services right away. Stage West's policy was to bring in television and movie stars to star for their productions. We had Joey Travolta, Donny Most from *Happy Days* (1974) fame, Barry William's from *The Brady Bunch* (1969) fame, and Johnny Crawford from *The Rifleman* (1958) fame. Each of those stars could sing and dance well. They were professional and a joy to work with. The rest of our cast included my wife, Charlene, and Dean Regan, who was one of the funniest actors I have ever worked with. He was also an accomplished tap dancer. Sherry Miller, a blond, statuesque, beautiful singer/actress from Toronto completed our star cast. It was a smash hit for Stage West Dinner Theatres.

By now, my marketing efforts at Cliff Cox's company were requiring more time. Sales were growing, which required more attention. DB Equipment Ltd. was becoming my mainstay of work. From 1992 through 2002, my show business work was becoming a secondary line of work. I continued to teach at Harbour Dance Centre, and adjudicate at dance festivals, but gradually I was spending much more time at DB Equipment Ltd.

In 1996, Charlene and I traveled to Toronto, Ontario, for our niece's wedding. From there we went on to New Your City for a brief holiday. I attended a tap class with Savion Glover, one of the best tap dancers in the world, and another with the Tap Dogs from Australia. We also saw two Broadway shows, *Bring in da Noise, Bring in da Funk* (1995) and *Forever Tango* (1996). *Forever Tango* (1996) was unique. The choreography was based on the Argentine Tango style and was very intense, sexy, and difficult to do. The unique thing about this production was that the cast was made of up of dancers from young to old, slim to large, and all were spectacular dancers. It was sensational!

The day before we were scheduled to return to Vancouver, Charlene and I were doing some shopping. As we were walking down Broadway, we spotted John Kennedy, Jr. walking towards us.

He was with another person, and they were deep in conversation. Whenever I see someone famous whom I have not met, I want to meet them. I did not want to miss the opportunity to meet with John Kennedy, Jr., so I urged Charlene to approach him. Charlene was just the opposite. She did not want to intrude or bother people. I was not going to let the moment pass us by, so I pulled Charlene over to him. He was a bit startled, at first, but after I introduced Charlene and myself, he relaxed and was so gracious with us. He talked to us for about twenty minutes. He said he was proud of the fact he had helped get more police on the streets of New York and, subsequently, the crime rate in the city was down. We were so excited that we did not even get a photograph with him, even though we both had our cameras with us. Magical, yes?

In 1997, I auditioned and was hired to act in the film *Angels in the Endzone* (1997), starring Christopher Lloyd of *Taxi* (1978) and *Back to the Future* (1985) fame. He was a gentleman, easy to talk to, and a joy to work with. This film was a sequel to the successful *Angels in The Outfield* (1951). I played one of the football player angels who helps a football player catch a touchdown pass in a championship game. I was working and doing what I loved to do. It was such a blessing!

Angels in the End Zone

In 1998, I was cast in the film *Wrongfully Accused* (1998), with Leslie Nielsen, Richard Crenna, and Kelly LeBrock. This movie was great fun, especially because we got to dance some authentic Irish dancing. Mairead O'Brien Kent, who was a member of the worldwide touring company of *Riverdance* (1995), choreographed this production number. Mairead had been teaching an Irish dance workshop at Harbour Dance Centre. She was in the studio next to my tap dance studio. Right there, in the hallway, she asked me to dance in the movie. I never even had to audition. What a great moment!

The premise of the production number was very funny. We shot the film on the Pacific National Exhibition fairgrounds, in the heat of the summer. Several of our local dancers, led by Kelly LeBrock, were cast as a SWAT team. They were dressed in full riot gear, with semi-automatic rifles. These costumes, with all the extra paraphanalia, weighed about thirty-five pounds each. The SWAT team characters would enter a town to free it from the grasp of a super villain. As they were about to capture the town, a larger SWAT Team, led by Richard Crenna, would surprise them, and order them to drop their weapons. When they refused to do so, the larger SWAT team would start shooting at their feet. In the ensuing chaos, they would drop their weapons and break into a frantic *Riverdance* (1995) routine. It was hysterical, but it proved to be dangerous. They shot plastic exploding pellets at our feet. Since Kelly LeBrock was not a dancer, I was placed next to her to help guide her through the routine. The way it was shot was the real treat. First, they shot it from the waist up. I was holding Kelly's hand by my side, and she followed my dancing. By bouncing when I bounced, she was Irish dancing. Next, they shot it from the waist down. Kelly was taken out of the shot and replaced by our choreographer, Mairead. For this shot, we were required to wear safety shields over our faces because the plastic pellets would explode, sending pieces of plastic flying all over the place. Protection for our eyes was most important. They matched both shots in post and final edit and it magically looked like Kelly LeBrock was doing all the Irish tap dancing that we were doing. Due to the summer heat and bulkiness and weight of the riot gear we were wearing, shooting this sequence was most uncomfortable. Even so, we had hysterical fun! Leslie Neilson was a most wonderful person. He was kind, compassionate, and made you laugh so hard your tears would run down your legs. Hah! After we finished filming our dance sequence, I went right back to DB Equipment Ltd., selling heating and cooling equipment.

In 2001 I landed a role in *The Swinging Nutcracker* (2001). This was a television special based on the *Nutcracker* (1982) ballet. It was directed by Shel Piercy and choreographed by Lisa Stevens. Our star was Canadian singing/dancing star, Jeffrey Hyslop. Jeffrey was one of the most talented performers in Canada. He was a bonafide triple threat. He was one of Canada's premier singer/dancer/actors. He could also choreograph, write, and direct. I played King Rat and had a duo of tap henchmen with me. One of them was Joshua Cyr, who became one of two Canadian tap dancers in the famous tap show *Tap Dogs from Australia* (1995). No small feat (pardon the pun)! On this show, I met dancer Paul Becker. He was hysterically funny! Paul Becker is now one of the top director/choreographers in the business. We had a ball!

In 2002, I had the honour of choreographing *A Very Merry Muppet Christmas* (2002), starring Joan Cusack, David Arquette, and the Muppets. I had heard about this opportunity from my current agent, Connie Hardy. I went to meet Jim Henson's son, Brian, at Lions Gate Studios on the North Shore. Brian was producing this wonderful Christmas movie. The meeting took only about seven or eight minutes, and they rewarded me with the job of choreographing the movie. They had heard of me during my time in Hollywood.

Choreographing this movie was a dream come true. I was thrilled to land this job. I had always loved the Muppets. What an experience! I staged two sequences for the film. One was an Irish tap dance for a rag tag bunch of Muppet musicians, Dr. Teeth and the Electric Mayhem. We shot this number similar to the way we shot the Irish dance sequence in *Wrongfully Accused* (1998). The procedure was remarkably interesting. We first shot the group of Muppets from the waist up, bouncing along to the dance steps. Next, we had the puppeteers lie on their stomachs, on a long table. They held only the legs of the Muppets. We shot from the edge of the table down, so all that could be seen were the legs and feet doing the dance steps. Finally, we matched the leg portion with the upper body portion, so it looked like they were really dancing. It looked great!

The next sequence we shot was the "Moulin Scrooge" production number, featuring Kermit, Miss Piggy, Pepe, three chickens, and a host of other Muppets. We shot it with the Muppets dancing in full frame. The dance floor was chest high to the puppeteers and, while they held their Muppets fully upright and put them through their paces, they referred to monitors below the floor level to make sure they were spaced correctly. It was quite an arduous process. Whatever action the puppeteers saw on their monitors they had to be done in reverse for the camera. You had to hand it to those wonderful artists and the magic they created. Those puppeteers were the absolute best in the business. Both numbers turned out wonderfully.

One of the most amazing things I had ever seen was during the filming of "Moulin Scrooge." On the theatre set, a bus full of children would arrive. The children would be brought onto the set. A break would immediately be called, and the puppeteers would get their Muppets and come into the theatre, where the kids were excitedly waiting. Then a phenomenon occurred. The puppeteers could be seen, by the children, holding the Muppets. The children began to talk to Miss Piggy, Kermit, and Pepe and they would answer the kids. When Miss Piggy and the others were required to go back to filming, the studio reporters asked the children if they enjoyed meeting Miss Piggy, Kermit, and Pepe. They said they did, but they did not remember the puppeteers at all, even though they had been holding their Muppets. The children saw and remembered only the Muppets. Phenomenal!

In 2003, I began teaching tap for Jennifer Bishop at her Rhythm Room dance school. I am proud to call Jennifer one of my best friends. She still has my adjudication remarks of her dancing, as a young girl, in a dance festival many years ago in Prince George, BC. I have enjoyed teaching at both of her studios for many years now. She not only hired me to teach for her, but she was helpful in furthering my career. Jennifer is not only a gifted tap dancer, singer, and teacher, she is one of the most loving, generous people I know. She is wickedly funny, compassionate, and humble. Her husband, Bill Costin, is a great pianist. We performed together many times. Her daughter, Olivia, is now thirteen and already tap dances, sings, and plays the piano like crazy. During Covid lockdown restrictions, Jennifer had to close one of her successful studios. Through her hard work and determination, her original studio has remained open and is now flourishing once again. Jennifer was, and still is, one of my angels.

Jennifer Bishop + Jim

Jennifer Bishop + Jim + Gig Morton

I started working full time in marketing and sales, with DB Equipment Ltd., in 2003. Any work that arose in show business was now my part time job. My efforts at DB Equipment were paying off and this work had become my main stay of income. In the evenings and at weekends, I continued to teach tap at Harbour Dance Centre and the Rhythm Room. Since my employer, Cliff Cox, was a professional singer we had the opportunity to perform and travel for company responsibilities. Mostly, wherever we travelled for business, we performed for the representatives who attended the conventions. We travelled and performed our eclectic show in Toronto, Ontario, Banff, Alberta, and New Zealand. We also travelled to promote the company's several types of heating and cooling equipment. We attended conventions, trade shows, and learning sessions all over the US and Canada. I was sent to Texas and Toronto to learn about Mitsubishi products. We also had many training sessions in Vancouver.

Cliff and I put together an eclectic performing troupe to have some fun and keep our show biz chops up. We billed it as Cox and

Company. Our show included Cliff Cox, who was an opera singer and musical comedy performer, his secretary, Lily Page, who was a current Vancouver Opera chorus member, my wife, Charlene, who was a theatre star in musical comedy, and me as the song and dance man. The troupe also featured opera singers Don Wright, Mel Erickson, and Marianne Barcelona, and a brilliant pianist, Robert Holliston.

During this time, I had great fun staging a dinner/restaurant show at a restaurant, in Gastown, called Sophies. Singer, Mel Erickson, from the Vancouver Opera chorus, and my wife, Charlene created several different shows for this venue. One show was a Gershwin songbook, one was a Cole Porter songbook, and there were many others. The pianist was the wonderful Lloyd Nicholson, followed later by pianist, Brian Tate. The restaurant had a lower floor, with a staircase in the centre of the room, which lead up to a seating area on the second floor. The shows were staged from the top of the staircase down to the bottom. It ran successfully for a couple of years. It was so pleasant to have a good dinner while being entertained by Mel and Charlene, accompanied by Lloyd Nicholson or Brian Tate on the piano. Occasionally, Cliff and other opera singers would join them and lend their voices to the evening's entertainment.

Since Cliff was involved with cricket and rugby when he was younger, he took us to New Zealand on two occasions. Once was for the International Cricket Festival and another time for the International Rugby Festival. Both times we performed our eclectic variety show, filled with opera, Broadway material, comedy, song, and dance. We had too much fun! New Zealand was a beautiful country. I had never seen the colour green that abounds there. On our day off, we took a trip to see the sights. We travelled north, towards Bay of Islands. Cliff had heard of an authentic *Crocodile Dundee* (1986) style of pub, tucked far away in the back hills. It truly lived up to its reputation. Not only were there cars parked outside, but there were also horses tied up. We felt we were walking into another time zone. The characters inside were just like you would see in the movie. The owner was very friendly, and as we talked, he soon realised we were performers. He said that we could not leave without some singing and dancing. From behind the bar, he pulled out what I initially thought was a gun but turned out to be a flute! Before we knew it, he was playing his flute and we were singing along. He had an old, upright piano in the bar, and he sat down to accompany us. He knew some opera and musical comedy tunes. He could play quite well, but the amazing thing was that he only played the black piano keys. He did not touch any of the white keys. He was such a character. Some of the guys had pistols strapped to their hips, but they were very appreciative. We were treated to so much booze, and unforgettable fun. I am still in awe at the experience. On the way back to Auckland, we took a tour of the first New Zealand governor's mansion. It was on an island a short distance from the mainland, and the ferry ride was gorgeous. On the way over to the island, we saw some penguins swimming in the water. The island and mansion were beautiful and there were pine trees and palm trees. It was so amazing. All the years working for Cliff were filled with company progress, fun, and joy.

I have maintained my teaching schedule throughout the years, and I had some wonderful things done for me. I performed on International Tap Dance Day every year. This was produced by The West Coast Tap Collective, headed by Jennifer Bishop. In 2004, I performed my solo tap routine for International Tap Dance Day, and I am going to tell you about this experience for the second time because I want to emphasize just how much it meant to me. On the evening of May 26, 2004, Jennifer Bishop and the West Coast Tap Collective presented me with a Lifetime Achievement Award for my Teaching and Choreography Contributions Internationally. I was thrilled, but there was more. Art Jones, Commissioner of Vancouver Civic Theatres, was in the audience and was called on stage. He presented me with the news that I was going to be inducted in the BC Entertainment Hall of Fame for Dance. This meant there would be an award ceremony at the world-famous Orpheum Theatre and my star would be embedded in the sidewalk in front of the theatre, just like the Hollywood Star Walk of Fame. Here is the kicker, my star is right next to my wife, Charlene Brandolini's, star for Music. Both are just one star away from Charlene's Uncle Foncie's star for his years of street photography on Granville Street. We are the only family to have three stars embedded in the sidewalk on Granville Street for the BC Entertainment Hall of Fame! Pretty amazing, no? That same night, recording artist Terry Jacks, was inducted along with me. Terry was a friend of mine. He wrote and recorded the worldwide hit *Seasons In The Sun* (1961). This was a spectacular honour for both of us. Jennifer Bishop generated both of my awards, and I am forever grateful. I will teach for her and support her in any way I can. I love her dearly.

Jim's BC Entertainment Hall of Fame star

I would like to say a few words about Red Robinson, Vancouver Radio jock star, and long-time friend. Red was a legend. Not only was he a big star in radio, but he also helped facilitate the careers of many of the music industries greatest stars, including Elvis Presley. All the stars who came to Vancouver were guests on Red's show. His studio, at CKWX, was the first 50,000-watt radio station in Vancouver. Red and I had known each other for many years. In 2006, Red was honoured, by the Gaming Commission, to have the show theatre at the new Hard Rock Casino named after him. It was named The Red Robinson Show Theatre. Red invited Charlene and me to join him for the opening night of the theatre. I was thrilled. He told me that there would be many people I knew attending. We assembled in the lobby of the theatre for cocktails and schmoozing. Red came up and said, "Come with me, Jim. I have someone I think you'll remember from Hollywood." We walked over to a man, who was standing with his back to me. Red said, "I think you might remember this guy from your past." As the man turned around, I immediately recognised him as Joe Esposito, road manager for Elvis. I had not seen him for at least forty-five years. He stared at me and said, "Jimmy Hibbard, what the f*ck happened to you?" We had lost touch with each other after the last Elvis film I did. We were so thrilled to see each other. We were like kids, yacking with each other. Joe told me that it was very unusual for Elvis to connect with anyone the way that he did with me. I liked Joe so much. He was the quintessential road manager and loved and took care of Elvis. What a moment for us, provided by the man of the evening, the humble Red Robinson. This was just the beginning of an amazing evening!

The headliner for the evening was Bill Medley, of The Righteous Brothers, and the opening act was Paul Revere and the Raiders. Wow, I was so excited! I had worked with both on *Where the Action Is* (1965). Paul Revere and the Raiders were the series house band, and The Righteous Brothers were frequent guest stars on the show. Red invited us to go backstage to see Bill Medley and Paul Revere and the Raiders. On the way, he introduced us to Wink Martindale, the game show king, and his wife, Sandy Ferra. Sandy asked me, "You don't remember me, do you?" I was embarrassed because I did not. She laughed and reminded me, "You and I danced together in the Elvis Presley movie, *Kissin' Cousins*," (1964). I remembered, then. We had a wonderful time on that film. By now, we had made it downstairs, and I noticed Paul Revere talking to someone in the hallway. As I approached, he looked at me and, after forty years, instantly recognised me. He exclaimed, "Why, Jimmy Hibbard! I knew you when you had hair." We laughed and laughed and had a great talk right there in the hallway. We both went to Bill Medley's dressing room, and Bill asked where I had been all these years. He was always so cool. It was a crazy night, made possible by the kindness and generosity of Red Robinson. Red was a great radio star. He was a gentleman, and a bonafide Vancouver legend!

Red Robinson + Jim

In 2010, Mitsubishi Electric took Cliff, his secretary, Lilly, Charlene, and me on a Caribbean cruise. This was a spectacular reward for my work marketing and selling the Mitsubishi heating and cooling products. In 2011, Cliff suddenly passed away. DB Equipment Ltd. went to his new, much younger, partner. This man was nothing like Cliff. Cliff was the heart and soul of DB Equipment Ltd. I decided to retire from the business and return to show business. I loved my time at DB Equipment Ltd., but I secretly longed to return to what I loved most. I realized, right away, that I could not work for the new owner in good conscience. Within a year, the new owner had destroyed the business, which Cliff had built up, and he closed the company down. I plunged back into looking for work in show business and, frankly, I could not have been happier!

I had always been so lucky to be in the right place at the right time, especially over my years in Hollywood. It was not just about being lucky. The more things you knew how to do, the more work you got. The risk of unemployment dropped considerably if you had varied skills. Like the phrase, Jack of all trades, master of none, I do not consider myself a master of anything, but I have learned many disciplines. With a desire to learn, the world begins to open. It certainly has for me.

In 2015, I was invited to audition for the movie *Descendants* (2015). This movie was directed and produced by the great Kenny Ortega. It starred four young actors, Dove Cameron, BooBoo Stewart, Cameron Boyce, and Sofia Carson. My participation was minor, but the story leading up to being cast as the museum guard is a good one. For fifteen years, I entrenched myself in teaching, choreographing, and performing as a solo song and dance man. I had concentrated on tap, which was my first love. My performing career in television and movies had taken a turn for the better. My friend and colleague, Paul Becker, invited me to the audition for *Descendants* (2015). He had posted a sign calling for dancers up to age of fifty. I reminded him that it had been quite a while since I saw fifty. He told me not to worry, that I could easily do the choreography. I relented and went to the audition.

There were around a hundred dancers waiting to try out for the movie, most of which were my tap students. We were warming up when Kenny Ortega and his entourage arrived. I had never met Kenny, as I had left Hollywood before he became a force in the business. Paul Becker's assistant choreographer, Louise Hradsky, taught us the dance combination and broke us into groups of ten. Kenny told us that he wanted us to dance the combo as demented actors under an evil spell. This was great! I loved this approach. It was right down my alley. My group was extremely excited, as was the case at any audition. I danced as dementedly as I could, resembling a character from Looney Tunes (1930). Suddenly, Kenny Ortega jumped up, came on the floor, and hugged me. He said, "This is the dancer of my dreams." He went on to tell everyone in the room, "If you want this job, dance just like this man," and instructed his entourage, "We have to find a part for this guy!" My head was spinning, and I had to remind myself that, while this was great, the praise should be taken with a grain of salt. I have had profusive praise a few times in my career and most of the time it did not pan out, for reasons beyond anyone's control. Anything may, or may not, happen in show business. Overall, it was extremely flattering, to say the least. Before we left, we had to face a camera, speak into a microphone, and state our name and age. We lined up and, as I got closer to the microphone, I started to think I should lie about my age. When it was my turn, I gave up and said, "I can't lie. My name is James Hibbard and I'm seventy-three years old." I thought that this truth might be the deal breaker, but Kenny stood up and said, "You're not seventy-three. No way. You can't be!"

Kenny Ortega + Jim, *Descendants* -Disney,
Bad Angels Productions, 5678 Production

This audition proved to me that you should never say never. I had truly stopped thinking about television and movies, because of my age, and I was concentrating on teaching, adjudicating, and choreographing competition numbers for dance festivals. Thanks to Paul convincing me to audition, I started working in television and film again. I gleefully credit Paul Becker with, single handedly, bringing me back into that work. Truthfully, I had never wanted to leave movies, television, and stage. I do not think I ever will.

Paul Becker

Paul told me that I would get a call with rehearsal dates. I was feeling particularly good about it. I did get a call from Paul, but it was with unwelcome news. Disney had cut the entire scene that we auditioned for. Paul told me he could give me three or four days in another dance sequence. A week later, Paul said he could not use me. I was seriously deflated, but then he told me it was because Kenny Ortega had found another part for me. Kenny followed through with what he had said at the audition. This was unusual in this business. Kenny kept his word, and cast me as the museum guard, in a sequence with the four young stars of the film. My scene with these four, beautiful kids took place in a museum, which housed several magical artifacts. My job was to look after them. The four stars would break into the museum, cast a spell on me, and, in a dreamlike state, I would move over to the magical spinning wheel. I would and touch the needle, with the tip of my finger, and instantly feel the need to sleep. Once asleep, the four kids would come in and steal a magic wand. They were too loud and woke me up. I proceed to chase them all over the museum. That was my silent cameo bit. I had great fun trying to believe I was Buster Keaton in a silent film.

After filming, I was invited to the wrap party and had a wonderful time. Kenny and I did some impromptu tap dancing together. Kenny Ortega was the real deal. In our careers we have worked with a lot of the same people but had never worked together previously. We had an exciting time telling each other stories of our lives in the business. I genuinely enjoyed every minute working with him.

The movie set site was the Parliamentary Buildings in Victoria, BC. We shot it throughout the night when the buildings were closed. Charlene and I made it a weekend get away with some shopping in beautiful Victoria, BC. We headed back home Monday morning. A great weekend!

From 2011 to 2015, I taught full time and performed each year for Tap Day. I also became busy adjudicating dance festivals in BC, Alberta, and Quebec. Each time I adjudicated, I began to realize more and more how much I loved being able to give back to young, aspiring dancers. I could do my part to let those artists know what it took to get to work with the best in the business, and to stay at that level. Teaching is the best profession in the world. It is my responsibility to help the next in line. It is the best I can do for or these young dancers/actors/singers. It brings me the ultimate pleasure. I remember each time a teacher, friend, or acquaintance, opened a door for me, and what a gift that was. Those gifts must be paid forward. I intend to do this every chance I get.

I would like to back track a bit. Years ago, in 1983, I was hired to be the entertainment director for Bud Kanke's new dance club, Confetti. The theme of the club was New Years Eve every night. I had several types of entertainment throughout each night. There were huge lineups of people to get into the club, so I had jugglers, magicians, and others entertaining the lineups outside. I had a gymnast, wearing an ape costume, inside. This ape would suddenly appear, swinging on a rope across the dance floor and up to the second level on the other side of the room. I had waitresses, who could do walkovers without spilling the drinks, serving customers. We had a confetti gun shoot, every hour, across the dance floor. We had a main stage act every night. I had contacted my good friend, Toni Basil, for her recommendation of an act suitable for the audiences of Vancouver. She had just discovered a wonderful dance group called the Cambellockers. This was one of the original street dancing crews. I had never seen lockers before. They were sensational, to say the least. I brought them to Vancouver for two weeks, to perform as headliners. They took Vancouver by storm.

Vancouver had never seen anything like them. We were at capacity, with steady audiences for the entire time they were here. I owe this wonderful experience to Toni Basil. She was one of the premiere dancer/choreographers in Los Angeles. She also recorded the hit single Mickey (1981). She had always been ahead of the time. She was a true visionary. I was her assistant choreographer on many productions while I was in Los Angeles. While the Cambellockers were in Vancouver, they graciously taught me some of their moves. While I was learning a few locking steps from them, I thought that locking and tap dancing would be a natural fusion of styles. I have kept working on it, from time to time, since then. My work fusing locking and tap dancing has paid off.

In 2012, I was asked to choreograph and dance a production number for a local dance troupe called the Vancity Lockers. Their leader was a wonderful dancer, named Kim Sato. She was a premiere locker and jazz dancer and was one of the best tap dancers I have worked with. She had also has been one of my past students. I should give some background as to why I was asked to choreograph them. Firstly, being asked to dance with them was an honour. They were one of the leading locking groups in Canada. They competed worldwide, with impressive results. Kim Sato had taken one of my tap classes, where I set the combo fusing locking with tap. Kim was extremely impressed and asked me to choreograph a number and dance with them. I staged the number and fused some tap work with locking. Kim and I did the tap work, and her crew took care of the serious locking. It may seem that these two dance disciplines would not blend well, but the result was a show stopping number which brought the house down.

After the show, Kim brought me on stage and presented me with a Lifetime Achievement Award, recognizing my ongoing outstanding achievements, excellence, and dedication to the art of dance. It was a beautiful, crystal sculpture. Kim, her stunning crew of five, and I had one of the best times of our lives. This was all Kim's idea from the start, when she asked me to set the number for her and her crew. Kim holds a place deep in my heart. I am humbled by the awards, and I will always be thankful.

I teach all my students that the more things they learn to do, the risk of being unemployed is lessened. This was a perfect example of that. I learned a little locking and was able to use it professionally. I teach my students that if you keep your chops up and get into class regularly, they will have the best chance of getting work. If they lose a job at an audition because they are not in shape, they have only themselves to blame. I tell me students to keep their noses clean, work harder than they ever thought they would, and not cause any friction. This will give them the best chance to be hired. A healthy, cheerful outlook is essential for success. Directors, choreographers, and producers will often hire based on attitude over talent. Those with negative or passive attitudes become known in the business and are quickly bypassed.

Back in 2002, Sas Sjelford founded the Vancouver Tap Dance Society. Sas, along with her assistant Anna Kramer, invited me to perform in their yearly productions for the International Tap Dance

Festival. These festivals were incredibly special occasions and celebrated the birthday of Bill Robinson (Bo Jangles). Similar shows are held around the world on or near May 25, every year! Local dance schools in every city take the opportunity to perform and learn from tap dance stars, who have created and nurtured the tap styles we enjoy today.

Sas Sjelford brought in incredibly special guest performers who were either tap dance legends or soon to be legends. This included our own local legend, Dr. Jeni Le Gon, who was the first Black woman to star in a film with Bill Robinson, and Diane Walker (Lady Di), America's first lady of tap. Other well-known names, such as Jimmy Slyde, legendary partner of The Slyde Brothers, Cholly Atkins, who also was a partner with the great Honi Coles, Brenda Buffalino, Heather Cornell, Terry Brock, Sam Weber, Lisa Anne La Touche, Travis Knights, Danny Nielson, Jason Janas, Bril Barrett, Jason Samuels Smith, Travis Knights and Aaaron Tolson were also featured. Lady Di, Brenda Buffalino, and Heather Cornell were tap dance historians responsible for reviving and perpetuating wonderful famous tap routines of tap greats such as Leon Collins, Steve Condos, the Copascetics, Eddie Brown, Honi Coles, Bunny Briggs, Sandman Sims, Pegleg Bates, Sammy Davis Jr., Buster Brown, Buck and Bubbles, the Slyde Brothers, and Eddie Green. Without teaching these routines to our young tappers, the dances would be forever lost. We owe them a great debt of gratitude.

Performing for the International Tap Dance Festivals, I shared the stage with those wonderful legends of tap. It was beyond humbling for me. Those legends, against great odds, have made it possible for every tap dancer to be able to do what they do today. I instruct all of my students to research the history of those great artists to understand how much work it takes to be successful, and to know who came before them and who paved the way.

In 2017, I was truly back in Hollywood again. My choreographer friend, Paul Becker, hired me to dance in two episodes of *A Series of Unfortunate Events* (2017), one episode of *Once Upon A Time* (2011), an episode of *Date My Dad* (2017), and an episode of *Psyche* (2006). I also danced on the television series *The Man in The High Castle* (2015), choreographed by my colleague, Richard O'Sullivan, and in a commercial for Crown Royal Whiskey, choreographed by Fatima and shot in Mexico City! It was certainly a busy time.

Jim *(Series of Unfortunate Events)* - *Series of Unfortunate Events,* Sonnenfeld Company, Paramount Television

In 2018, I auditioned for a remake of the movie *Freaky Friday* (2003). The assistant choreographer was Louise Hradsky, who had worked on all of Paul Becker's jobs. She remembered me and let the choreographer, John Carrafa, know that I would be trying out. I got the job and had a blast working on it. I was seventy-five years old, and it was a humbling experience to be dancing with people half my age or younger. John's choreography was challenging and rewarding. He was so respectful of my work. Movie director, Steve Carr, let me know that his favourite dance number of all time was the Waiters Galop from the movie Hello Dolly (1969), which I had danced in. He had downloaded the number onto his laptop and played it over and over on set for all to see. In *Freaky Friday* (2003), there was a scene where several featured waiters proceed to the floor and remove tables and chairs at a furious pace. John Carrafa's choreography of this piece rivaled the Waiters Galop. It was exceedingly difficult choreography, conducted by our sensational dancers. It was extremely exciting to watch. John was such a talented man, and a true gentleman. I loved working with him on this film. During filming, I was also keeping up with my teaching and adjudicating responsibilities.

John Carrafa and dance crew (*Freaky Friday*) - *Freaky Friday* - Disney Channel, Disney +

Soon after finishing filming, I got a call from my agents, Melissa Panton and Shannon Teat, at daCosta Talent Agency. I had been offered the job of reprising my museum guard role, for *Descendants 3* (2019). Kenny Ortega would be directing and producing again, and this was such a great compliment! Kenny, the producers, and crew welcomed me back. I spoke with Kenny on set and thanked him for requesting me. He told me that it was not just him, but also Disney Studios had asked if I could come back. They could have used anyone, but they graciously hired me again. This was very unusual in this business. I still believe Kenny had more to do with me getting this role than he let on. It was just the kind of guy he was.

We shot my scene in the Parliamentary Buildings in Victoria, BC once again. It felt like old home week with family. It was a night shoot, starting at 10:30pm and ending at 5:30am. My scene was like the previous one, opening with me falling asleep while a witch turns off all alarms and has her way in the museum. I had great fun catching up with Kenny and hearing about his numerous current and upcoming projects. We did a little impromptu tap dancing together, on a break from filming, and at the wrap party. Once again, Charlene, came with me for the shoot and we had fun doing some more shopping in beautiful Victoria, BC. The next day, at 3:00pm, we were on a ferry headed home. I love this business!

By the end of 2018 I had been blessed with another professional job on the theatre stage. Every job seemed to come unexpectedly, but I believe that if you are positive and keep working hard at your craft, nurture your friendships, and stay humble, people will think of you from time to time. My angels always remained with me and looked out after me. This opportunity proved that this was the case. Many years prior, I had choreographed and played a lead role of Lucky for the Arts Club Theatre production of Dames *at Sea* (1966). I was subsequently brought back, by Bill Millerd, to choreograph the second production of Dames at Sea. In that production, the lead role of Dick was played by a young upcoming performer named Peter Jorgensen. We became good friends during the run, but we did not have the opportunity to work together for many years. Peter became a working director and writer and formed a production company called Patrick Street Productions. He and his wife, Katey Wright, adapted and produced *It's A Wonderful Life* (1946) for the stage, and Peter directed it for stage four times. He consistently improved the show. This adaptation was fabulous. It was the result of hard, creative, positive work. Peter and Katey have done us all a great service. Their funny, poignant story was full of love, hope, and understanding of our fellow man. These are qualities we should embrace more than ever right now, with the current discord in the United States, Canada, and the world. Patrick Street Productions was the only professional company in BC to only produce musical theatre productions, and to provide a living wage to all of the performers.

After many years, Peter Jorgensen did think of me and asked me if I would be interested in being in the show. I met with him at his home, read some lines, and sang a little for the role of Uncle Billy. This role was played by the famous actor, Thomas Mitchell, in the movie version. I immediately loved the role. The character was around sixty-five years old, and was a loveable uncle to George Bailey, the starring role. Uncle Billy was the character who lost their savings and was an alcoholic. This was a multi-level role where I got to sing, dance, and test my acting chops. It was a dream role, really. Kayla Dunbar was the choreographer of note. The only number Kayla did not choreograph was my solo song and dance feature. This was George and Ira Gershwin's song *Nice Work If You Can Get It* (1937). Peter put together a superb cast for the show and his direction was insightful and right on the money. It was full of beautiful voices, good actors, and dancers. The lead role of George Bailey was played by Nick Fontaine, a superb actor and singer. The timber in his voice was very much like that of James Stewart's speaking voice. The female lead role of Mary Hatch was played by Erin-Aberle Palm, a young, up and coming star, with a beautiful voice. Clarence, the angel, was played by the superb Greg Armstrong Morris, who could not have been more type cast. He was truly a pixelated angel in person. At the first rehearsal, it was evident that our collective heart was there. Everyone was fully into it and committed. This was rare. We had a great extended rehearsal schedule, of a full week, on the superb set design by Brian Ball. Having extra working time with the set, props, lighting, and sound, along with the added gift of an eleven-piece live orchestra, was a rare experience. The musical director, Angus Kellet, had worked with me on many theatrical productions at the Arts Club Theatre. He was a joy to work with.

The show was performed at the Gateway Theatre, a superbly designed theatre with a professional crew, who were committed to the project. The houses were great, and we ran until December 31, 2018. I was sad to see it close. I had such a fun time. This show was timely. With all the turmoil in the world, this show spread the message of hope and togetherness to bring us all to a better place. I was lucky enough to receive a Best Supporting Actor nomination from the Theatre Ovation Awards Committee. I did not win, but that did not matter. The compliment was plenty.

The year 2019 picked up where 2018 left off, screaming full speed ahead! With some encouragement from my wife, I decided to find a talent agency to represent me with the new work that was coming my way. I spoke with some actors and dancers, who also felt this was a good move. It made sense. In Los Angeles, you needed an agent to get into auditions, and business in Vancouver had grown to that point. I put my feelers out to find an agency I would feel comfortable with. It turned out to be daCosta Talent Agency. They represented not only actors, singers, directors, and writers, but also many dancers and choreographers. I met with Melissa Panton and Shannon Teat and sealed the deal. I was a bit reticent, but they were gracious, knowledgeable, and made me feel wonderfully comfortable. It had been a long time since I had agency representation, but this felt like a good fit. It has worked out well. They are good at what they do, and I would recommend them to anyone. They are very professional, indeed.

In 2019, I had the opportunity to travel to London and Italy. This opportunity arose thanks to Susan Skemp and Richard McBride. I had directed and choreographed a production of *Anything Goes* (1934), for Theatre Under the Stars, in 1987. This production starred both Susan and Richard. Since then, Richard has become a producer, and Susan his co-producer! Richard has a website called La La World, which is an entertainment, news, video, and blog type show, as well as a Youtube channel. He is full of bright, fun energy.

Susan and Richard asked if I would be interested in having a filmed interview. For this filming, they had secured a private room just off the lobby of the Douglas Hotel, in Vancouver. It was professionally set up, with three cameras rolling simultaneously. Susan was the main interviewer, with Richard occasionally adding questions to the mix. They were very well prepared. Susan had my life and resume, in chronological order, down to a tee. It was a wonderful day. It took about three hours to complete. They proposed to produce a television series of master class reunions, with me reconnecting with stars I had worked with previously, such as Julie Andrews, Barbra Streisand, Goldie Hawn, Toni Basil, Ann- Margret, and Nancy Sinatra.

Around this time, Barbra Streisand was about to give a concert in Hyde Park, London. Richard and Susan asked if I would be interested in seeing the concert and meeting up with Barbra. I jumped at the opportunity. Richard took Charlene and me to London but, unfortunately, Susan was unable to join us. We had a spectacular time! Charlene, Richard, and I went to Barbra's concert in Hyde Park. She was in fine voice and gave a wonderful performance. Sadly, we were not able to meet with Barbra after the show. We visited Buckingham Palace and saw the Changing of the Guard, Covent Garden and the Theatre District. We were also fortunate to take in a stage production of *City of Angels* (1989). Thanks to Richard McBride's extreme generosity, Charlene and I then took the opportunity to travel on and visit Rome, Italy, for four spectacular days. We had never visited Rome or London before, so this trip was glorious. We saw the Trevi Fountain, the Colosseum, the Vatican museums, the Sistine Chapel, and the Spanish Steps. Very impressive! Words cannot fully relate the formidable beauty of those sites in Rome. We met up with Richard after our jaunt to Rome and had another couple of days in London. You need to be in the presence of Richard McBride to understand how vibrant he is!

I was so impressed with Richard McBride. He was a force, full of crazy energy and ideas. He was a fledgling producer who put his money where his mouth is, a rarity these days. It is wonderful how relationships created many years before can morph into moments like this. Never say die! While Richard and Susan have since parted ways, I am forever grateful for his generosity in providing Charlene and me with the trip of a lifetime. I am currently working with Susan on my book, along with other projects we are creating. It is extremely exciting. More good things are on their way.

Shortly after, news came out that producer/director/choreographer Kenny Ortega was coming back to Vancouver to audition dancers for his new television series *Julie and the Phantoms* (2020). He was executive producing, directing, and co-choreographing the series. Paul Becker would be co-choreographing the series and would have the opportunity to direct some of the episodes, for the first time in his career. This would be a spectacular break for him!

Kenny Ortega + Jim. *(Julie and the Phantoms) - Julie and the Phantoms,* Bright Light Pictures, Cross Over Entertainment

The audition was held at Bridge Studios, in Vancouver. I had not been at a big-time audition like this since auditioning in Hollywood in the 1960s. There were at least four hundred and fifty dancers there. We were grouped according to age and held outside the soundstage.

When Paul Becker arrived, he and I had a great reunion. Kenny's flight was late, so we were forced to wait a while longer. When he finally arrived, he came right up and hugged me. He whispered in my ear that he had an acting/dancing part in mind for me. He told me that I was his muse! All his projects, that I had been in, had been super successful. What a wonderful thing for him to say, and for me to hear. To say I was enthusiastic would be an understatement. The studio had built a huge, raised, sprung dance floor with mirrors running the entire length of the soundstage. I felt like I was back at 20th Century Fox. It was impressive! Since there were so many dancers of varying ages, I knew this audition would take many hours.

The assistant choreographers for the production were Louise Hradsky and Victoria Caro. Louise was a petite, powerhouse dancer and a superb assistant. She had her feet on the ground. She knew exactly what she was doing and was extremely talented. Victoria Caro was cut from the same mold. She was all business, very pulled together, and a superb dancer who could tumble with the best of gymnasts. They taught us an extensive dance combination for the show. It was long, fast, and exceedingly difficult. When it was set, they broke us into groups of twenty-five and started the weeding out process. Paul, Louise, and Victoria would run us through the routine and then we would sit down while they watched the next group. During this painstaking process, Kenny was elsewhere taking care of other business. When it was our turn to dance again, they would call out the names of the people they wanted to stay and the rest of the dancers in the group would pack up and leave. This weeding out process was time consuming. Several hours passed. When all the dancers they liked had been chosen, Kenny came in to watch. We went through the combinations many times for him. He started to make suggestions of how to film the dances, and his ideas were refreshing. The dance combinations were already good, but he took them, mushed things around for camera purposes, and made it come alive. He and Paul were very clever, multi-talented men.

Towards the end of the audition, which by now was five hours, Kenny congratulated us. He came over to me and told me that he wanted me to play the role of the janitor at the junior high school. I would have the opportunity to do some tap dancing, singing, and to recite some lines. I would also have a scene with the young star of the series, Madison Reyes. I was going to sing and dance with dancers half my age and younger. This was starting to become a trend. This was going to be great fun! I would also get to sing and dance along side my friend, Craig Hempsted, who was a phenomenal dancer. Craig was chosen to play one of the teachers at the school. Steffanie Davis, another of Canada's spectacular dancers, was also selected. All the dancers chosen were among the best in the country. As I mentioned, this audition was just like the big-time musical auditions I went to in Hollywood!

The star of *Julie and the Phantoms* (2020) was Madison Reyes. She was quite the find, and the making of a real Hollywood story. Kenny auditioned her in New York and signed her on the spot. She was new and had never auditioned before, let alone worked. She sent Kenny her audition tape and the rest is modern movie making history. Wonderful things do happen! She was a phenomenon! She sang, danced, and acted up a storm. Her energy was infectious. The room lit up when she entered it. The story centres around The Phantoms, three members of a boy band, who had been dead for twenty-five years. They help Julie find her passion for music and life. She, in turn, helps them become the band they were never able to be. These co-stars were all incredibly talented as well. In real life, they sang, danced, and played instruments. All the dancers were wonderful. I felt fortunate to be in my 70s, dancing with these babies. I was absolutely blessed. Rehearsals were a joy, with fast and furious choreography.

The episode was filmed at St. Edmonds Catholic School, in North Vancouver. It was the same school my son attended, which was a cool thing. The school had closed because a new school had been erected next to the original. The dance number was set to a song titled *I Got the Music* (2020), and it took place all over the school. It was set in classrooms, hallways, on the stairs, in the music room, and the finale was in the gymnasium. In one scene, I push Julie down the hallway on my janitor's cart. The cart was very heavy and, in addition to pushing it down a long hallway, I had to dance behind it, spin it fully around, do some featured tap dancing, and sing at the same time. We rehearsed and rehearsed this scene, got it ready to shoot, and then Kenny suggested that we shoot it from a different angle. This meant doing my featured tap dance section on the other foot. Fortunately, I had a lot of experience with transposing on the spot. The dancers and choreographers were worried that I would have trouble. I have had to change on the spot before and assured them it was not a problem. I promptly did the tap dance combo on the other foot. They were incredibly surprised with the ease at which I did this. It was natural for me. When I leaned how to dance, I had to do everything on both feet. After all this, Kenny decided to shoot it from the original angle, anyway. Show business, you have to love it! My scene with Julie went smoothly and we were finally done. The whole dance number, with scenes, took twelve full days to rehearse and shoot.

Jim as Janitor *(Julie and the Phantoms)* - *Julie and the Phantoms*, Bright Light Pictures, Cross Over Entertainment

Kenny Ortega was one of the most talented people I had ever worked with. His credits would take up a couple of chapters. To list a few of his accomplishments, he has directed *Newsies* (1992), directed and choreographed *Hocus Pocus* (1993), directed the *High School Musical* (2006) trilogy, Michael Jackson's *This Is It* (2009), and executive produced, directed, and co-choreographed the *Descendants* (2015) trilogy. In 2019, Kenny received his star on the Hollywood Walk of Fame. His mentor was none other than Gene Kelly. One of the things Gene taught Kenny was how to use the camera to shoot dance sequences. At the time, it was ground-breaking. This knowledge, coupled with his own spectacular talents, has led to Kenny becoming a giant in the business.

Kenny and I have become great friends. Every time we get together, we start swapping stories. We shared similar backgrounds and worked with many of the same people. Kenny and I have shown off our tap-dancing skills and done some impromptu dancing together. Working with Kenny Ortega was a major gift! Not only is he an immense talent, but he is also one of the kindest humans I have ever met. He loves artists. He is a born mentor. He remembers where he came from. He remembers how hard it is to succeed in this business. His work ethic is unquestioned. If you ever get the gift of working with Kenny Ortega, you will fall in love with him

The entire dance world knows Mandy Moore. She is the critically acclaimed, Emmy Award winning choreographer with wonderful credits to her name. On February 22, 2019, I auditioned for her, on a new NBC/LionsGate production of a television series called *Zoey's Extraordinary Playlist* (2020). I may be seventy-five years old, but my spirit does not know that. Do not spill the beans. Fortunately, for me, my body is holding up. I am truly blessed. I am still ready to thump and bump! Every working dancer in Vancouver was at the audition. Jillian Meyers and Jeff Mortensen conducted the audition. Jeff was a friend of mine and one of Canada's finest dancers. I had worked with him on a couple of Paul Becker's projects. We gathered in studio two, at Harbour Dance Centre. There was electricity in the air. Jeff and Jillian greeted us as we warmed up and waited for Mandy to arrive. When Mandy arrived, she introduced herself and told us what the show was about. We then waited until they finished setting up the sound equipment. I walked right up to Ms. Moore, told her my name, and said I was incredibly happy to meet her. I told her I was a fan of her work. She came around from the back of the table, hugged me, and said that it was a thrill to meet me. She had heard about me from the dance community in Hollywood and from her assistant, Jeff Mortensen. She told me, right then and there, that she had looked forward to working with me and that we should go lunch sometime soon. She wanted to pick my brain about my time in Hollywood. She was so charming! She made me, and everyone else, feel very relaxed and you knew she had your back. It gave everyone confidence. This was a rare quality and she had it in spades.

Jeff and Jillian taught the dance combination. It was fun, fast, and difficult. I had a wonderful time, learning and dancing the combo. The choreography was difficult, natural, and great fun. I was a little out of practice at auditioning, so I had to a little work to do in picking up the dance combo. Fortunately, for me, I was in the last of twelve groups. This gave me some extra time to get it down. The dancers were very respectful of my experience, and my being more that twice their age. Two of them offered to run it with me, which shows the generosity of dancers. I thank dancers, Scotty Augustine and Joanne Pesusich, for their help. To me, dancers are the kindest, most helpful, and most supportive people in show business. They have, what I call, the dancers heart. I had seen it a thousand times. At an audition, every dancer wants to get the job but, at the same time, they will help other dancers to learn the combination. This is not found with other artists in the business. I do not mean to suggest that other artists are not great people just that it does not usually happen. The dancer's heart is just the coolest thing!

Dancers understand the struggle of picking up the combo quickly, harnessing, and dancing it, full out! The thrill is spectacular. Your soul is fed and your soul soars. It is incredibly special! I have worked with, taught, and worked for dancers my entire career. Dancers are the most supportive, compassionate, helpful people in the business. Dancers understand how hard you must work to be a professional. The camaraderie among dancers is unique.

Mandy Moore and her associate choreographers, Jillian and Jeff, seemed very pleased with my audition. Jillian said I was the only dancer with perfect rhythm. This was a genuinely nice compliment. I was pleased with what I did, and it had been great fun! They took videos of every dancer and said there would be lots of work to come. When the pilot episode they had shot in San Francisco was picked up by NBC, they would start casting the dancers from Vancouver. I did what all dancers do after they audition. They wait and wait.

While waiting to hear from *Zoey's Extraordinary Playlist* (2020), I got a call from Paul Becker. He wanted me to play a character in one of the production numbers in his new film project *Good Boys* (2019). I would play an older man in a food court, harassed by precocious boys. We shot the number in a food court in a mall. It was great to work with Paul again. It was also great to work with fellow dancers, Scott Augustine, Craig Hempsted, JoAnne Pesusich, and Mark Samuels again.

Following this, Louise Hradsky, who works as Paul Becker's assistant on most of his projects, was signed to choreograph the movie *To all The Boys: PS, I Still Love You* (2020). She asked my agents to submit me for the part of Bud, a member of a posh retirement home. I would be required to dance in many scenes and act, without lines. The director took a liking to me and gave me some lines on the day of filming. I had a really fun time. Louise Hradsky was very gracious in thinking of me for this job. It was one of those lovely moments you never forget.

Good to Mandy Moore's word, my agents got a call from Ms. Moore, requesting me to dance in an episode of Zoey's *Extraordinary Playlist* (2020). I was thrilled. I reported to rehearsal, at a food court in Tsawwassen, BC, with forty-nine other dancers! The number was a controlled flash mob, who help Zoey's love interest profess his love for the star of the series, Jane Levy. It was a blast and a half! Mandy and her assistants, Jillian and Jeff, were very well prepared. There was no lost time here. All fifty dancers knew what we were required to do in record time. We filmed the sequence in the scheduled time and both the director and Mandy complimented me on my performance. This was very classy, indeed! That evening, I watched the pilot episode of the series. I really liked the show.

Since then, Mandy has hired me to sing and dance in another episode of the show. In this episode, I play a priest. The number takes place in a mortuary. There are eight dancer/singers, Zoey, Zoey's mom and brother, and three mortuary staff members. Zoey's mother, played by Mary Steenburgen, sang lead. I am a Steenburgen fan, and it was great to meet her. She was gracious and fun to work with. We were all in the mortuary to choose a casket for our separate situations. The song we sang was *We Got To Get Out Of This Place* (1965), by the Animals. It was such a strange setting to do a song and dance, but it worked very well. We all really wanted to get out of that place. It was fun to do a dramatic song and dance. I can not say enough how talented, organized, and lovely Mandy Moore was. Equally as lovely and talented were her assistants, Jillian Meyers and Jeff Mortensen. Working with Mandy was like going to show business heaven. It was immediately evident that she respected and supported you. I hope to work with her again.

The year 2019 was scorching by. It felt like the same, exciting energy was in the air as it was in Los Angeles in the 60s. My agents, Melissa Panton and Shannon Teat, told me that I had been requested, by Kenny Ortega and Paul Becker, to record some lines and sing on my episode of Julie *and the Phantoms* (2020). At a recording studio, near Lionsgate's North Shore Studios, I was sat on a stool in front of a microphone and large screen. There was a phone next to me. On the phone were Kenny and Paul, talking to me from Los Angeles. They told me what they wanted me to say for lines, and then the technician would prompt me at the right time. I had done this before in Los Angeles. It was the same as the foley work that I had done, recording all the various sounds of horses' hooves, people walking and dancing, thunderclaps, and rain, all set to the music. They had me sing the song from the dance number we had already shot. I had an enjoyable conversation with them, and Kenny was excited that the series was picked up for a second season. They would be back in Vancouver to start shooting in May or June, and I was in their plans.

Shortly afterwards, I heard that Peter Jorgensen was planning to remount *It's a Wonderful Life* (1946) at the Anvil Centre Theatre in New Westminster, BC. With this production, Nick Fontaine, Erin Aberle-Palm, Gregory Armstrong Morris, and I would return along with veteran actor/singer Steven Aberle as the villain, and one of Canada's leading triple threats in the business, Colleen Winton, as Mrs. Bailey. This production was again, a joyous experience. After our fun at the Anvil Theatre our whole world as we know it changed forever with the introduction of a worldwide pandemic.

2020 marked the most terrifying development in all our lives. The advent of the very deadly disease, Novel Corona Virus (Covid-19). By the end of 2020, there were 346,000 people in North America who had died from it. The entire world was suffering. People were asked to stay at home, self distance, and wear masks. Work in show business went into lock down. Every dance school I taught at closed, the television and movie industry were shut down, my work with the theatre arts students at Capilano University was at a stand still, every outlet was closed. Only essential services were functioning, such as hospitals, grocery stores, police departments, and fire departments. Front line workers were working, exhaustively, to treat those who contracted the disease and attempting to save the lives of those who had to go on ventilators. Many of those on a ventilator did not come away alive. It was very scary, indeed.

There were some positives. People communicated more with family and loved ones using social media platforms. Creative teachers gave virtual dance classes from their homes, studios, outside on the street, and in parks. I was able to give virtual dance lessons from a couple of the dance studios I taught at, and some from my home. It was challenging, but necessary. Although it was a scary time, I trusted in our medical experts and knew that if we could survive until a vaccine was discovered, we would be able to return to a new normal existence. I learned to never take anything for granted again. The Pandemic has shown how fragile our existence is. I hope we do not forget to continue to take great care of ourselves and others as much as we did during the worst times of Covid-19. Too many people were so impatient, wanting to congregate, refusing to wear masks or gloves, and not social distancing. While we desperately needed to get some sense of normalcy, we needed to do so with respect for our fellow human beings. The most positive result of all that has happened is that the Earth is healing itself. Pollution was down, and clear water was coming back to the canals in Venice. My friends in Los Angeles were thrilled to not have to deal with smog and told me there had been stretches of weeks on end of clear skies. What a change.

The virus struck great terror in every artist's heart. Our only hope was to try to stem the spread of it, by simply wearing a mask and staying home. One of the most tragic developments of the pandemic was the damage, globally, to the arts business. Movie and televsiion productions were shut down, theatres were closed, young dancer/actor/singers, who have worked so hard to reach the level where they can now step out and make a name for themselves, ran into a Covid brick wall. Some became highly creative, but the outlets that were available to them before were no longer there. For economical reasons alone, they were forced to work in other types of business just to survive. Time was not on their side. We did not know how long this would last. I have been blessed to be able to have had a wonderful career. My heart broke for those young artists. For some it would be easy, for some it would be hard, for some it just would not happen. Martin Luther King once said, "A change is gonna come." Well, that change certainly came.

The great news soon emerged that Pfizer, Moderna, and Johnson and Johnson had produced vaccines with high efficacy ratings. Most people quickly scrambled to get vaccinated, but there were still a percentage of people out there who refused, for one reason or another. Living with the virus is now part of our normal life. Fortunately, the vaccines have helped to combat the virus and prevent people from becoming extremely sick and dying.

On the home front, the Covid restrictions gave me time to stay at home and devote my energy toward authoring this book. My good friend, Susan Skemp, and my family have been so helpful and supportive. My love for all of them is firmly intact and even more pronounced. I began teaching again at Harbour Dance Centre and at the Rhythm Room. Their safety protocols were solid, and social distancing was possible. At least the studios could stay afloat. It was certainly challenging to adjust to this new normal.

Gradually, the movie and television projects started up again, which was good news. Thanks to their extremely strict testing and mask wearing protocols, the safest work environment was on the sets and locations. Under Covid restrictions, I worked on *Batwoman* (2019), *Julie and the Phantoms* (2020), *Motherland: Fort Salem* (2020), *Peacemaker* (2022), *The Last of Us* (2013), and *Grease: Rise of the Pink Ladies* (2022).

During the early days of Covid, my agents asked me to video myself doing various facial expressions for a new video game. This would be a new experience for me. I knew a lot of colleagues who had done it for movies, television, and games, but I had never done it. I arrived at the studio and met the technician. He put black dots all over my face in the outer office. We went into the studio, and I sat on a stool inside a circular cage, with what seemed like fifty cameras pointed at my face. It was very cool. Some might feel claustrophobic in that space, but I love new experiences. We proceeded to shoot around eighty different facial expressions. I had a metal rod as a headrest against the back of my head, so that I would stay the same distance away from the cameras. I had to hold my head steady and not look up or down. It was a very exacting process and, when we were finished, about two hours later, I was truly exhausted. Yet I was exhilarated having never done this before. Wonderful day!

The Last of Us (2013) was a new television series, scheduled for release in 2022, for HBO MAX. The episode I worked on was directed by Neil Druckman, the author of the video game the series is based on. Choreography was by Paul Becker with Victoria Caro and Paul Becker's daughter, Marlee Grace Becker, as associate choreographers. My character was an infected citizen with immense fungi on my face, head, and neck, being controlled by some unseen force. I was part of a select group of thirteen dancers from Vancouver, Los Angeles and Calgary. The production company spared no expense. They flew all thirteen of us to Calgary and back for one day of costume fittings, before rehearsals and filming were scheduled. Amazing! Every time I have worked with Paul, it has been first class all the way.

We had two makeup artists, each, assigned to create their designs on us. My two makeup artists were thirty-five-year-old identical twins. They finished each other's sentences. They were so in tune with each other as they applied the fungi on me. They created a masterpiece. It took them five full hours to apply the fungi, and another two and a half hours to remove. This had to be done from scratch on two separate shooting days. The first day of shooting had us dancers, and twenty-five extras, writhing and rolling around on a big mound of dirt and moss, outside, in freezing weather. It was uncomfortable, to say the least. The second shooting day had all of us storming a building, seeking out anyone living to annihilate. We had to jump over dead bodies, slide through blood, and run through gasoline on the floor, while trying to get to one of the female stars of the show. The scene ended up with us being burned to death when the woman, to save herself, threw a lighted match on the floor and engulfed us in flames. I loved it. The entire rehearsal and shoot took seven full days. What an extraordinary experience! Working in such an extensive prosthetic build up was a first for me. It made profound sense to hire dancers to lead the attack because dancers are used to moving amazingly fast, in many different directions at once, and still hit marks at the right time. All good dancers are good actors, as well.

Jim in *The Last of Us - The Last of Us,* Naughty Dog, Playstation Productions, Sony Pictures Television

Jim in *The Last of Us - The Last of Us,* Naughty Dog, Playstation Productions, Sony Pictures Television

Grease: The Rise of the Pink Ladies (2022) was a Paramount Studios Television project, choreographed by Jamal Sims, with Louise Hradsky and Jeffrey Mortensen assisting. The period was early 1950s, before the play and movie. Once again, I was honoured to be chosen as one of six dancers to play a role as a club founder in the building where Rydell High School would become. We were dressed in turn of the century tuxedos. Marisa Davila, who plays the lead role of Jane, gets shown a painting of us and we suddenly come alive and sing and dance with her, explaining the requirements of joining our club. When we had our portrait done it was around 1900 and we were older gents who were successful, arrogant, and quite racist. It was funny, edgy, and the girl was overwhelmed by us. We learned the whole number in four hours. We rehearsed two more times the next week and shot the number on the following day. On shoot day our call was 4:00am and we finished around 8:30pm. Sixteen-hour days are not unusual in this business. It was a long day, but worth every second of it.

Since we were to look like a painting done in the early 1900s, the time it took for hair and makeup to look exactly as the painting took about three hours. The hair and makeup artists were highly skilled. It took at least an hour and a half to remove their creations. For days afterwards, I was removing paint from my fingernails and from out of my ears. Our day of filming took over sixteen hours. We did not get to see the results, but production seemed incredibly happy with what they filmed. I was tired, but it was that good, tired feeling you get when you know you have done a good job.

This was my first time working with choreographer, Jamal Sims. He was a lovely man, very relaxed, and prepared. He also expressed his respect for me in front of everybody at the end of rehearsal. I was so surprised. He made me feel incredibly special. It was a truly kind, gracious thing to do. I was humbled by his remarks. Even Marisa Davila, the director, Diego Valasco, the crew, and the director of photography expressed genuine respect for me. The other dancers and I were well taken care of and had great fun. I loved every minute of it, and I was exactly where I wanted to be.

My editor and partner, Susan Skemp, and I plan to produce a television series with the same name as my book, "Can't Stop Dancing." I will be the host. I am going to present dance disciplines of every description, including tap, ballet, street, contemporary, jazz, cabaret, and heels, from all over the world. My guests will be dancers, director, and choreographers who have made their mark, those who are making noise, and those who deserve to be seen. We will have regular dancers who are capable of many disciplines, and we will add featured performers as we go. Each show will feature our dancers in rehearsal, through to a complete, fully choreographed, costumed, and lighted dance sequence. Sometimes I will lead the dancers, sometimes my guest artists will lead them. We will be able to meet artists from all over the world. We will have a chance to talk to and learn from them. I am extremely excited and will keep you all posted.

I am seventy-five years old now, doing what I love to do. To quote Noel Coward, "What could be better than that?" I have been using Facebook to promote my endeavours for some time and it has been a Godsend. I do not tell folks what I had for breakfast or any personal stuff, I just tell everyone what I am doing, in television, movies, stage, and teaching. It has put me in contact with my great friends in Los Angeles from all the years of performing there. People I never knew, who are fans of my work, have made themselves known to me. I never knew they were out there. For me it is heart warming, to say the least, and I am humbled by their comments. My life has been full of wonderful events and now I am in touch with my friends and people who shared those experiences. Facebook has become my PR representative, and my friend.

Canadian Work In Chronological Order:

1972 - relocated to Canada

1973 - *Dames at Sea* - Arts Club Theatre
    Worked with competitive ice skaters
    Taught at Synergy Dance

1974 - 1975 Worked with competitive ice skaters

1975 - 1976 - No 5 Orange

1976 - *Wolfman Jack* - CBC

1977 - 1978 - *Rene Simard* television series - 2 seasons - CBC

1977 - 1980 - *Canadian Express* television series- CBC

1977 - 1978 - *Starting Here Starting Now* - Stage Revue - Art Club Theatre, Vancouver, Belfry Theatre, Victoria, BC, Stage West Dinner Theatre-Calgary /Edmonton w/George Chakiris

1979 - *The Raes* - CBC

1980 - *Pippin* - Arts Club Theatre

1981 - *By Design*, movie w/Patty Duke

1982 - *The Pyjama Game* – Theatre Under The Stars

1982 - *Paul Anka* television series - CBC

1983 - *Godspell* - Vancouver Playhouse

1983 - *Cabaret* - Arts Club Theatre

1983 - *In Motion* - First Choice Cable Fitness Series - w/professional dancers

1983 - Super Socco - Power Drink Commercial

1984 - *Guys and Dolls* - Arts Club Theatre

1985 - Peace Keeping Tour - Canadian Armed Forces

1986 - 2011 - DB Equipment Ltd

1987 - *Anything Goes* - Theatre Under The Stars

1987 - Peace Keeping Tour # 2 - Canadian Armed Forces

1988 - *Little Shop Of Horrors* - Theatre Under The Stars

1989 - *Little Shop Of Horrors* - Arts Club Theatre

1989 - *Best Little Whorehouse In Texas* - Theatre Under The Stars

1990 - *I Love My Wife* - Arts Club Theatre

1991 - *I Love My Wife* - Stage West Dinner Theatre

2002 - *A Very Merry Muppets Christmas* movie

2003 - Tap Day - received Lifetime Achievement in Teaching and Choreography from West Coast Tap Collective

2004 - Inducted into the BC Entertainment Hall of Fame for Contributions to Dance

2005 - Cox and Co.- Toronto, Ontario

2006 - Cox and Co. - Banff, Alberta

2007 - Sophies Dinner Club, Vancouver, BC

2008 - Cox and Co - New Zealand

2009 - Cox and Co - New Zealand

2010 - Caribbean Cruise - Mitsubishi Industrial

2011 - Left DB. Equipment Ltd

2012 - Lifetime Achievement Award from Urban Alchemy

2013 - teaching, Tap Day performing, Adjudicating

2014 - teaching, Tap Day performing, Adjudicating

2015 - *Descendants* movie - Kenny Ortega director

2016 - teaching, Tap Day performing, Adjudicating

2017 - *A Series of Unfortunate Events* w/ Paul Becker, Choreographer

2017 - *Once Upon A Time* w/ Paul Becker, Choreographer

2017 - *Date My Dad* - w/Paul Becker and Louise Hradsky, co-choreographers

2017- *Psyche-* w/ Paul Becker, Choreographer

2017 - *Man in High Castle* w/Richard O'Sullivan, Choreographer

2017 - Crown Royal Apple Commercial in Mexico City, Mexico w/ Fatima, Choreographer

2018 - *Freaky Friday* movie

2018- *Descendants 3* movie- Kenny Ortega

2018 - *To All The Boys I've Loved Before* movie w/Louise Hradsky, Choreographer

2018 - *It's A Wonderful Life* - Gateway Theatre - w/Peter Jorgensen, Director

2019 - *Zoey's Extraordinary Playlist* - 2 episodes w/Mandy Moore, Choreographer

2019 - *Julie And The Phantoms* w/Kenny Ortega, Director and Paul Becker, Choreographer

2019 - *Good Boys* movie

To All The Boys I've Loved Before movie

2019 - *It's A Wonderful Life* - Anvil Centre Theatre - w/Peter Jorgensen, Director

2019 - *Zoey's Extraordinary Playlist*

2020 - *Julie and the Phantoms*

Zoey's Extraordinary Playlist

ADR - *Julie and the Phantoms* - voice over - Automated Dialog Replacement

Holland - motion capture for a game. Graham Qually

Batwoman - TV series. Produced and directed by Holly Dale

2021- *Motherland: Fort Salem*

2021 - *Peacemaker*

2021 - *The Last of Us*

2022 – *Grease: The Rise Of The Pink Ladies*

Chapter Twenty

My Family

My wife, Charlene Hibbard (nee Brandolini), is a talented singer and actress. We will have been married for fifty-eight years on October 15, 2022. The jury is still out as to whether she will keep me, but I think I have a good chance. I have talked about Charlene many times, not only because she is my wife, but also because she has starred in all the productions I have directed or choreographed. We have performed together many times. If you do not have your A game when you are on stage with her, you are simply left in the dust. She is a truly a funny lady. She thinks funny. Charlene is a perfectionist and always is at the top of her game. She is as funny as Lucille Ball, Mary Tyler Moore, Carmen Miranda, Gracie Allen, and any other of our funny ladies on screen or stage. She is equally as good. The very moment I met her in the summer of 1964, I fell in love with her. I just knew she was the girl for me.

Jim and Charlene dancing

Jim and Charlene

Charlene and Jim

Most of Charlene's family live in Vancouver and Kelowna, BC, Canada. Charlene's mother's side of the family are from the South of Italy, a province called Calabria, and her father's side of the family are from the North of Italy, a province call Udine. She grew up very close to all of her grandparents, aunts, uncles, cousins and extended family members. She recalls, fondly, of getting together every Sunday at their homes or at different parks or picnics. Most of my extended family still live in Idaho. My family's heritage is all English and Irish. My family is not as numerous as Charlene's, but we were just as close while growing up. As with most families, as they grow and begin to spread out, we do not get together now as much as we would like to.

Charlene Hibbard's Kitchen Dance

Charlene is a great cook, but she would not agree. I like everything she prepares, so my word counts. She learned a great deal from the Italian women in her family, and she has a passion for cooking. Charlene has an extraordinary eye for fashion and style. We have several closets filled with her clothing and shoes, and I have a three foot by seven-foot space in one closet that has all my clothes so firmly packed that I don't have to worry about pressing anything. My shoes are neatly piled on top of each other. I really do not mind; this is the way it should be. Charlene is also an exceptionally talented interior designer, without any training in that field. She has exquisite taste and, of course, is creative. Our home is beautiful, and, at Christmas time, our house could be featured in a magazine. You should see her doing her kitchen dance as she prepares dinner, it is breathtakingly funny. She retired from performing sometime ago, but every time she sings with that beautiful voice, I begin to cry. She is the love of my life, and my best critic. She keeps me grounded. Her honesty is unquestioned, and her character is above question. She is everything that is good. We are best friends, and our arguments have a vibrant life to them. She is my Missus, and I am her Mister.

Our son, Jason Hayes Hibbard, is the youngest of two children. He was born in Los Angeles on June 3, 1971. He weighed thirteen pounds, nine ounces. He was so fat; we did not see his big eyes for several weeks. Jason is one of the kindest, most compassionate, loving people I know. Jason is now six feet two inches and is tall, dark, and handsome. He has been married twice and has a child from each marriage. His eldest is Havana, who is now twenty-four years old and is a strawberry blond beauty. She is working successfully in television and movies in the Health Protocol services area. His second child is Furious Hayes Hibbard, who is now fifteen years old. Jason named his son Furious after a character in the movie *Boys In The Hood* (1991). The star was Lawrence Fishburne, who played a father with great strength and commitment to his son. Jason was so impressed with Fishburne's character, Furious, that he named his son after him. Once, while Charlene and I were vacationing in Mexico, we were told that the literal translation of the name Jason is "protector of children." This describes our son to a tee. He is happiest when he is with his children, and he is a protector of children everywhere.

My son Jason Hibbard

My grandchildren Furious, Havana with their dad, Jason Hibbard

Jason has worked in show business and is a talented, funny, writer. He has written a screenplay for a superhero movie, which we hope will one day be produced. He is entrepreneurial and is currently working for a real estate company, called Properly. It is owned by the television stars, the Property Brothers. I once thought he would follow in my footsteps as a dancer. Jason attended a Catholic school and, when he was nine years old, he asked me to come to his school for show and tell day. He had been getting some tap lessons there. I went to the school and met his two teachers, Sister Josephine Marie, and Sister Mary Lucinda. Neither were over four feet ten inches in height. I was sure they must have played Munchkins in the *Wizard of Oz* (1939). They sat me down and the class took the floor. The teachers lifted their habits and both were wearing tap shoes, with ribbons tied in bows. They gave me a wonderful presentation of their tap work. I have to say my son was incredibly good and showed natural talent. I took my shoes with me, and I had such a fun time tapping with them. This made me think he wanted to become a dancer like me, but it was not to be. Nevertheless, it was an experience I will never forget. I am immensely proud to say that Jason, my son, is my best friend.

Our daughter, Gianna Francesca Hibbard, is the eldest my two children. Gi was born in Los Angeles on July 12, 1966. Both of our children are still landed immigrants. Gi is all of five feet tall and is a beautiful bombshell. She has the spirit of a wild horse. She excelled in school. When she was ten years old, she was hit by a speeding pickup truck in the lane behind our house. She was returning to school on her bike, after coming home for lunch. Charlene and I were working at the time the accident occurred and Charlene's Aunty Elma was doing nanny duties for us. Charlene's older brother, Leon, picked her up and drove her to Lions Gate Hospital. Aunty Elma called me, and I left my rehearsal and drove to the hospital. By the time Charlene and I got there the first thing we were told was that Gianna would not make it through the night. We were stricken with terror! It is every parent's worst nightmare. We stayed with Gianna through the night and were advised to make plans for the worst. Against all odds, Gianna did make it. With her will to live and help from our angels, Gi is still with us. All these years since the accident, the road to recovery has not been easy. She was severely injured.

She had brain stem damage and some broken bones. She had to learn to walk, talk, and eat again. Doctors really did not know what the effects of the injuries would be, or how long they would last and to what extent. It has been a constant struggle, especially for Gi, all these years. You can imagine how difficult everything was for her. It was also extremely difficult for our son, Jason, because of all the attention Gianna's recovery process demanded. Through it all, she has pulled through well. She married and gave birth, and raised our first grandchild, Sterling James. She lives within fifteen minutes of our home, and we get to see her all the time. Gi is a vibrant, spiritual soul and we love her with all our collective heart.

My daughter, Gianna Hibbard

I must tell you about my grandson, Sterling. He is now thirty-one years old. Several years ago, Charlene and I noticed he was always drumming his hands on the kitchen table, or anywhere, for that matter. We thought he might like to learn to be a drummer. As a birthday gift, we gave him a set of drumming lessons at a place called Tom Lee Music. He really enjoyed the lessons, so we bought him another session. From that point on, he has paid his own way and is now one of the most gifted drummers I have ever seen. He has worked hard, bought his incredible drum sets, and is a member of a popular progressive metal band called Kosm. They have recorded a few albums and I have had the pleasure to attend a few of their concerts. He is truly a magnificent performer. When you watch his band, your eye goes immediately to Sterling. He is a vibrant showman! He subs his talents out to other bands for gigs or studio recordings. He is also teaching steadily.

My grandson, Sterling Paterson

We are truly blessed to have our beautiful family, with the added bonus being that they are all within fifteen minutes of our home. We get to see them whenever we need to, which is most of the time. Not bad at all!

Chapter Twenty One

Looking Back

As far back as I can remember, I have always had a positive nature. I have never given any time to negative or passive thoughts. I knew my parents and my extended family loved me. My childhood was full of wonder and fun. I learned to fish at the age of four and was rarely without a fishing pole in my hand. My dad was a logger, so I was always in the woods. Those woods were my church, of sorts. I never felt any danger. Seeing bear, deer, elk, rabbits, and every other kind of animal was usual fare. My dad taught me at an early age that if I minded my own business, and listened more than talked, I would be fine. I was, and I am to this very day.

After watching Gene Kelly, Donald O'Connor, Cyd Charisse, Dan Dailey, Michael Kidd and Debbie Reynolds strut their stuff on the silver screen, I knew that whatever they were doing, I wanted to do it, too. I did not know why, then, except it made me happy and it made all the people watching me feel the same. I liked the attention I got and I still do to this day. My mother and her friends encouraged me, but my dad and my brother could not understand my attraction to dancing at all. Even though my dad did not know why I loved to dance, he paid for my training, which is something. Through all these years I have heard so many stories from male dancers who were teased and bullied because they wanted to dance. I do not remember being teased by classmates or anyone else. From the beginning I was so committed that I did not recognize anything but support. I remember that I could not wait to dance. I loved classes and practicing. I craved the positive audience response. The applause was so gratifying and still is. I remember, so distinctly, the joy in the eyes and faces of children and adults confined to hospital beds. I would tap dance around their beds. They could not clap, but they showed their appreciation by smiling and the happiness in their eyes was wonderful.

It was natural for me to practice every day. I never really thought about it. I just did it. I knew I was improving quickly, and I liked the feeling. Without knowing it, I was developing respect for myself that would carry me throughout my life. I love the audience. I love being on stage under the lights, whether it be in the theatre, in front of the camera, in night clubs, or when teaching. My love for performing, whether it be dancing, acting, singing, choreographing, directing, producing, teaching, or adjudicating has grown and is as vibrant to me now as it was from the beginning.

You do not get ahead in this business without help. I have talked about this many times, but it bears repeating. Your parents, teachers, family, friends, workmates, colleagues, and fans all contribute to your success. You must remember these people. I consider them as my angels. Remember the doors they opened for you. You honour them by working harder than you ever thought you would or could, keep your nose clean, do not make waves, and remain positive. When you are positive, directors, choreographers, and colleagues will want you in their productions. There have been times when I got a job when I was not as good of a dancer as someone else. I was hired because of my reputation as a hard worker, and someone who worked well with every company. If you are negative, you will become known as a potential liability, and this reputation will get around quick.

I recall twice in my career when I achieved a new level of my dancing ability, while doing shows. The first time was during the first production of *West Side Story* (1957) in 1964. We had several people in the production who had done the play on Broadway and in London and were also in the movie. They knew all the original Jerome Robbins' choreography and direction. In those days, any company who wanted to do the production had to stage Jerome

Robbins' original choreography. It was in Jerome Robbins original contract. When I learned the difficult choreography and was able to do it well, I became a much better dancer, and I knew it. The choreography and direction were so perfectly constructed. When you continued to do it well, you kept improving throughout the run of the show. The second time I had such an experience was in the rock opera *Tommy* (1969) in 1971.The choreographer was Claude Thompson, who was a premiere danseur with the vaunted Alvin Ailey Dance Company. The choreography was so demanding of every technique I had ever learned about dance. I had never danced his style before. I learned and danced it well, and I knew, from that moment on, I could dance any style thrown at me. These were two levels of dance expertise that I accomplished that were harder than the last, but so gratifying to reach. It also made me remember and cherish the great dance training I have had from so many gifted teachers.

Each level of dancing expertise you attain will get harder and harder, but the rewards are greater and greater. I remember the only time I ever got negative remarks from a teacher. It was in Los Angeles, shortly after I arrived there. She was a guest teacher at Nico Charisse's school, where I was training. She took me aside and told me, "You will never be an accomplished professional dancer. You have flat feet which will keep you from jumping high. You are not tall enough." I proved her wrong! Let me tell you, no one has the right to ever say anything like this to you. No one has the right to step on your dreams. I must have told Nico what she said to me, because she was gone from the school the very next day. When someone like that has the nerve to say something like this to you, it is only to make themselves feel more powerful. They are bullies! Remain positive. You will attract people of a like mind. Nothing can stop you. You will get stronger and stronger. One thing is very sure, I have worked hard my entire life. Learning to dance, with the discipline it takes to become good, requires consistent work at your craft. You have to work harder than you ever thought you would have to. If you do, you will improve faster than you ever thought you could. Learn as many unique styles of dance as you possibly can. The more things you learn to do, the less the risk of unemployment. Learn tap, jazz, ballet, contemporary, ethnic styles, hip hop, and other forms of street dancing. Take on anything that interests you. You name it, I did it. I even studied mime work for a while in Los Angeles and, years later, I got a featured spot on a television special as a mime. You just never know.

I started working consistently by the time I was seventeen years old. As my jobs continued to grow, I felt as though it was a natural course of events to get the amount of work I did. I felt that if you worked hard enough at your craft, you would get the work. In truth, I am blessed. I have had a wonderful career, and I am still working! What could be better than this? Looking back, drafting my story has reminded me that no-one can do it alone. Remain humble. Know that you are talented but thank your lucky stars that you are. If you are fortunate enough to be doing something you love to do, you will never work another day in your life.

Here is a truth that I have learned through my years. We think we have time, but we really do not. When I was young, I thought summers and school years would never end. It is clear to me now that time does speed up as you get older. Keep your chops up by staying in class on a regular basis, especially when you achieve some success. When you do, you will always be ready when an opportunity arises. If you do not keep your chops up, and you lose a job, you have only yourself to blame. The opportunity may not come again. You know the phrase, "If you don't use it, you will lose it." It is brutally true. On the flip side, play hard with the same discipline that you train with. Be nice to yourself and congratulate yourselves with your achievements. Stay humble and be kind. When you realize your dreams, remember who helped get you there. And, if it is in your nature, take time to help the next one in line.

The question most asked of me is, "Throughout your career, what is the most favourite job you have done?" My answer surprises some people. Every job I have ever done is my favourite job. I feel the same about every project I do, whether it is in movies, television, stage, nightclub, teaching classes, or private lessons. Each new endeavour is just as important as the last. No matter with whom you are working, whether it be a famous star or a student, it is equally important to everyone that you simply do your best. When you have done an excellent job, the result is the same. I have always felt this. Simply be the best you can be for everyone. Always treat every person you meet with dignity and respect. Do not take anyone or anything for granted. There is no free ride. If you make working hard and smart the usual, it ceases to be work. You really do not have a lot of time. Do not waste one-second of it. Passive and negative thoughts and actions take you where you do not want to go. Positive energy always brings you to better places. I am getting preachy, so I will just say, "Get up, get out, and thump and bump, because the alternative stinks!"

I certainly have not been an angel all my life, but I have been blessed with a positive outlook. I never give up. I fight gravity every day, and I am surrounded with love from family and friends. Here is some advice. Develop a bag of tricks to keep in your toolbox. Every time you see a performance, a dance work, a movie, or a concert, or just have an inspiration, put all the exciting moments that impressed you in your memory bank, which becomes your toolbox. You do not have to repeat the work of others but take them and put your own creative spin on them. It is okay to steal, respectfully, and them make it your own. Tap dancers have done this for generations. Remember that everything has been done, before you came along, but maybe not the way you would do it. At some point, due to time restrictions, being exhausted, or having a dry creative spell, you may choose to not give something your all. As an example, there have been times when I chose to finish some choreography with simple moves anyone could do, just to get it done. Other times, while performing, because of being tired or creatively dry, I did not do my best. These are the times when you can revisit your toolbox for one of your tricks to help you finish with a flair worthy of your work.

There are incredibly talented people who have written my life's philosophy in songs that resonate with me now. One is a song written by Lori McKenna and first released by American country music singer, Tim McGraw. It is called *Humble and Kind*. These words are in my heart and mind every day. This song is my life's mantra!

Lyrics to *Humble and Kind* by Lori McKenna/recorded by Tim McGraw

You know there's a light that glows by the front door

Don't forget the keys under the mat

Childhood stars shine, always stay humble and kind

Go to church cause your momma says to' visit grandpa every chance that you can

It won't be waste of time

Always stay humble and kind

Hold the door, say please, say thank you

Don't steal, don't cheat, and don't lie

I know you got mountains to climb

Always stay humble and kind

When the dreams you're dreamin' come to you

When the work you put in is realized

Let yourself feel the pride but,

Always stay humble and kind

Don't expect a fee ride from no one

Don't hold a grudge or a chip and here's why

Bitterness keeps you from flying
Always stay humble and kind
Know the difference between sleeping with someone
And sleeping with someone you love
I love you ain't no pickup line so
Always stay humble and kind
When it's hot eat a root beer popsicle
Shut of the AC and roll the windows down
Let that summer sunshine
Always stay humble and kind
Don't take for granted the love this life gives you
When you get where you're going
Don't forget to turn back around
And help the next one in line
Always stay humble and kind

My mother was my first and everlasting angel. She made sure that I had the opportunity to realize my dreams. It is wonderful to be able to help someone else realize their dreams. Take these words and put them into motion. Do not let up for a second. Be good to yourself, recognize your successes, and celebrate them. Remember, as you grow older, life seems to speed up. Make each moment count. Be kind and show compassion. Accept gifts graciously and be generous with your gifting. You know we are all here, not for a long time, so make it a good time. Be the best you can be, so the word regret does not become part of your vocabulary. Every person who ever helped you in any way are your angels. Honour them and they will be with you every day of your life.

All my life I have worked hard to achieve my dreams. I love dancing and dancing has been exceptionally good to me. I know my life has been blessed, and I also recognize my responsibility to honour it. I am not an expert in anything. I am proud to say I am still a student. I am living proof that you can do whatever you set your mind to. To this day, I am still dancing, and, to my everlasting benefit, I can't stop dancing.

Love and Ciaofornow - Jim

Angels never to forget:

Charlene Hibbard (nee Brandolini)

Gillie Brandolini

Ermie Brandolini

Lois Hibbard

Mike Hibbard

Sheril & Bobby Freedman

Forest Ivan Hibbard

Nico Charisse

Zita Charisse

Roland Dupree

Trudi Ames

Walter Painter

Anita Mann

Pam Freeman

Lesley Evans

Pete Menefee

Michael Schwartz

Jill Gordon

Susan Skemp

Nanette Charisse

Gene Nelson

Miriam Nelson

Toni Basil

Onna White

Rini Jarmon

Alex Plasschaert

Bobby Thompson

Lou Procopio

Barbara Luna

Jerilyn Stapleton

Dick Humphreys

Elvis Presley

Joe Esposito

Clancy Grass

All my dance students

Bill Millerd

Peter Jorgensen

Lelani Marrell

Colleen Winton

Stephan Aberle

Nick Fontaine

Erin Aberle Palm

Michael Kidd

Shelagh Hackett

Jim Hutchison

Goldie Hawn

Earl Barton

Paul Becker

Kenny Ortega

Louise Hradsky

Jeff Mortensen

Jillian Meyers

Every director I've worked for

Bob Sidney

Joe Leighton

Buddy Schwab

Harry Brandolini

Leon Brandolini

Aunty Elma

All my family members

Jason Hibbard

Gianna Hibbard

Havana Hibbard

Furious Hibbard

Sterling Paterson

Phil Feldman

Edward Feldman

Norman Browning

Jay Brazeau

Jerry Adolph

Pamela Rosa (nee Quick)

Craig Hempsted

Victoria Langton

Danielle Clifford

Jennifer Bishop

Bill Costin

Bruce Kellet

Bob Tucker

Lillian Winger

Delores Winger

Roberta Tennes

Cliff Cox

Patsy Macdonald

Mike Watt

Ken Gibson

Hugh Pickett

Jeffrey Hyslop

Ruth Nichol

Rae Ackerman

Timmy Tam

Shannon Teat

Melissa Panton

Connie Hardie

Mike Ward

Hazel Macmillan

Valerie Easton

Mary Lou Brien

Shirley Kozak

Jackie Coleman

Art Jones

Shirley Hibbard

Sheila Grosso

John Carafa

Marc Samuels

Kate Kahn

Kenny Loggins

Tom Jones

Rene Simard

James Angels

Bill Henderson

David Winters

Ann-Margret

Wayne Shulman

Suzanne Charney

The Kim Sisters

Anne Murray

Leon Bibb

Michelle Simmons

Claude Thompson

Ted Neeley

Frankie Avalon

Jack Cassidy

Mickey Rooney

Jack Benny

The Lennon Sisters

Teri Hatcher

Mandy Moore

Dick Clark

Sparky

Gillian Barber

Keri Minty

All my Capilano students

Frank Sinatra

Nancy Sinatra

Trudi Ziskind

Edith and Lou Ziskind

Paul Wallace

Peggy Fleming

Dick Foster

Joe Tremaine

Toni Sinclair

Sam Moses

Susan Anderson

Steffanie Davis

Bill Allman

All the dancers I've ever worked with

Bobby Rydell

Victoria Caro

Alex Pesusich

Joanne Pesusich

Kvyn Burgsma

Marianne Barcelona

Don Wright

Lilliane Page

My high school English teacher

Pat Proud

Garry Chalk

Rosanne Hopkins

Bert Michaels

Bobby Banas

Tommy Banks

George Chakiris

Mary Tyler Moore

Julie Andrews

Carol Channing

Maria Ghava

Gus Trikonis

Alan Thicke

Tommy Cahill

Susie Birstein

Dean Regan

Shel Piercy

Marcus Mosley

Blu Mankuma

Cecilly Day

Lesley Uggams

Natalie Wood

James Burrows

Brian Avnet

Bobby Elwart

Groucho Marx

Larry Fine

Brian Keith

Cyd Charisse

Nick Charisse

Joy Ciro

Paul Revere and the Raiders

Cherrill and Robbie Rae

Candus Churchill

Sibel Thrasher

Dennis Simpson

Larry Lillo

Diane Arnold

Jim Bates

Jackson Davies

Tamara Thompson Levi

Gregory Armstrong-Morris

Susan Lehman

Bobby Kirkwood

Dana Walden

Candy Moroz

Debbie Wakeman

Marlowe Windsor

Nathan Fadear

Sammy Davis Junior

Diane Walker

Jason Samuels Smith

Jason Janas

Jimmy Slyde

Cholly Atkins

Teri Garr

Jonathan Lucas

Jack Baker

Lisa LaTouche

Savion Glover

Danny Nielsen

Brent Carver

Lucille Ball

Donald O'Connor

Maurice Kelly

Jack Donohue

Andre Tayir

Gene Kelly

Bea Lilly

Ross Hunter

George Roy Hill

All of my Facebook friends

Mickey Rooney

Jack Cassidy

Bert May

Toni Charmoli

Andy Thoma

Louis Armstrong

Maggie Banks

Barbara Luna

Tom Hatten

Red West

Norman Browning

Laurie Peyton

Bobby Van

Ron McDougal

All my tap students

Brian Keith

Belinda Sobie

Jamal Sims

Kevin Tookey

Navid Sharkh

Greer Whillans

Danielle Clifford

Rusty Frank

Michael Whelan

Bobby Kirkwood

Joanne DiVito

Michelle Bernath

Ann-Margret

Dianne Arnold

Kathy Kroll

BearManor Media

Ben Ohmart

Shelley Stewart Hunt

Mary Lou Brien

Patsy Macdonald

Scott Augustine

Melina Rounis

Fred Astaire

Tony Charmoli

Lisa Billett

Stephanie Collard

Brenda Buffalino

Robert Wagner

Alice Faye

Phil Harris

Ross Hunter

Sam Feldman

Francis Ford Coppola

Leigh Torlage…